con gli occhi et con l'intelletto
Explaining the Tarot in Sixteenth Century Italy

Edition, translation and commentary by
ROSS SINCLAIR CALDWELL,
THIERRY DEPAULIS,
MARCO PONZI

2018

The authors are especially grateful to Giordano Berti, Claire Lesage, Franco Pratesi, Girolamo Zorli, and the team of Tarot History Forum, for their assistance and inspiration.

ISBN 978-0-244-67169-3
Second edition

Published and printed by Lulu.com

TABLE OF CONTENTS

Introduction

In 1980, Professor Michael Dummett's book *The Game of Tarot* (see Bibliography) brought a totally new approach to the history of the Tarot. It also gave an impulse to further research, particularly in Italy, the recognised birthplace of the game. Franco Pratesi, a professor of Materials Science from Florence, was one who had heard the call. He knew that the many and rich libraries of Italy were to yield treasures.

In 1986 he started publishing in *The Playing-Card*, the journal of the International Playing-Card Society, a series of memorable articles under the general heading "Italian cards: New discoveries". The second article of this series, titled "An early praise of Italian tarot in the 16th century", appeared in February 1987.[1] In it, Pratesi claimed to have found a 16th-century manuscript that praised the Tarot, whereas until then we knew only of texts that condemned it (like the late 15th-century sermon published by Steele). Pratesi's find was a real treasure-trove. As our readers will see, it offers many insights into the Tarot, but from a non-esoteric point of view. It also sheds some light on the way the game was played at the time and in the place where the anonymous author lived. As Pratesi rightly stated, it follows the "B" order of trumps, that is, the order which was used in Ferrara. (It is our Discorso 2.)

Some months later, after publishing his third article – dealing with F.A. Lollio's *Invettiva... contra il giuoco del taroco* (1550) and its unpublished (and hitherto unknown) *Risposta* by one Vincenzo Imperiali – Franco Pratesi published a fourth, called "Tarot in Piedmont in the XVIth century: the oldest book on the subject".[2] This was about a printed book, Piscina's *Discorso sopra l'ordine delle figure dei Tarocchi* of 1565 (our Discorso 1), which was actually so rare that for centuries its date was mistakenly given as 1570. How Pratesi managed to find the only copy that is preserved in a public library, he did not say. In 1986, when he did his research, there were no online cata-

---

1 Pratesi 1987a.

2 Pratesi 1987c. Franco Pratesi was not finished with his "Italian cards: New discoveries" series with this 4th article. Six further contributions were to appear until 1989, some quite important. They were followed by other articles in the 1990s.

logues. Anyway, he had to cross Piedmont to the remote town of Borgomanero (Province Novara) where this copy is kept. The article gave a summary of the book, pictures of the title-page and of the beginning of the text, and some thoughts about the strange, half-C, half-A trump order which the author used.

This new find led Dummett to speak very highly of the discoverer in a short article again published in *The Playing-Card*.[3] He underlined the importance of Piscina's *Discorso*, adding that "the Discorso reveals a trump order which, alone among those of which we know, has mixed affinities." Significantly Dummett echoed the Piscina discovery whereas he had not done so for the, perhaps more important, discovery of the anonymous *Discorso*. It seems Piscina provided Dummett with such good evidence for his theory about the influence of Bologna on Piedmont, that the other text appeared, at least in his eyes, less exciting. Dummett has written almost nothing about the anonymous *Discorso* in his later works on the Tarot. It is our purpose in this book to bring this rare text into the light and make it available. It has been unjustly overlooked until now.

The texts offer strange similarities. They are nearly contemporary, as we show of the anonymous *Discorso*. However, they cannot have influenced each other: Piscina's book was published in southern Piedmont, probably in a very small run (hence its present extreme rarity), and its circulation may not have gone far beyond the limits of the Savoy States, while the anonymous *Discorso* never seems to have been printed at all. As Franco Pratesi has remarked, it is a "B-type" Tarot trump order, and therefore must have been written in a Ferrarese context. But both texts address the meaning of the Tarot trumps and the suit cards from a variety of interesting perspectives. Drawing from philosophy, religion, poetry, contemporary science, and the rules of the game itself, while at the same time offering examples from history and current events, both authors describe a series of images that for them is more than a game. They find that the symbolism of the cards, and their order, offer moral lessons and a wholesome guide to the ultimate purpose of life, which is to seek God.

These two documents provide a valuable addition to our understanding of the place of games in the human imagination. Games are not only a social pastime, they offer the opportunity to ponder the structure of society and the meaning of life. With these discourses, Tarot takes its place alongside previous moralities of Chess and regular playing cards, along with the ubiquitous

3 Michael Dummett, "Correspondence", *The Playing-Card*, Vol. XVI, no.2, Nov. 1987, pp. 65-7.

dice, as a symbol of the vagaries of Fortune, as another avenue of reflection on the human condition, and the concerns of people of their time and place.

These two discourses are the earliest ever written, and offer a rare glimpse into the other side of the game of Tarot in its first centuries – the meanings educated people might have seen in the pictures on the cards.

The three present editors thought it would help Tarot researchers to give a complete edition of these two texts, the first extremely rare, the second being printed here for the first time, together with a translation into English and the necessary annotation.

Comparison

		Anonymous	#	Piscina		
		Perfection of number Four : having in itself three, two, and one, it comes to include ten, which contains all other numbers.				
		Meaning of Tarocco: a tasty sauce				
		Meaning of the Court Cards				
	The four suits	Denari: riches				
		Spade: military life				
		Mazze: political power				
		Coppe: gluttony and pleasure				
		Meaning of Trionfi: affects and passions that triumph on men				
Active Life		Matto: Foolishness	0	Matto: the joker who appears at the beginning of a comedy, the beginning and the end of human life, the sign of the Inn of the Fool	The Inn of the Fool	Things that are subject to Fortune / Things that are subject to Death
		Special game rules about the Fool				
		Bagattello: a juggler, symbol of the deceptions of the world	1	Bagato: the Innkeeper of the Inn of the Fool		
				Special game rules about the Fool. Meaning of the Court Cards		
	The highest dignities in the spiritual and in the temporal	Papa col Regno	2	Imperatore	High Princes	
		Papa senza Regno / Cardinale	3	Imperatore		
		Re	4	Papa		
		Imperatore	5	Papa – an Emperor can sometimes win over a Pope		
	Virtues desired by many	Prudenza: virtue of the soul, perfection in all sciences	6	Amore: Cupido, Vulgar Love	Things that mainly pertain to the High Princes	
		Fortezza: virtue of the body	7	Giustizia: follows Love because Justice must be free from passion		
	Three most powerful human affects	Amore	8	Carro Triomphante		
		Carro	9	Fortezza		
		Fortuna	10	Fortuna		
		Gobbo: time and old age	11	Vecchio Gobbo: a prudent counsel		
		Traditore: deceptions of the murderous world	12	Impiccatto: a dishonest and vicious man		
		Morte	13	Morte: the extreme evil		
Contemplative Life		Diavolo: the miserable end of those who follow foolishness as their guide	14	Temperanza: stands for all other virtues that do not fear Death		Things that are not subject to Death
	The supernatural creatures of God	Cieli: the Skies	15	Demoni: intermediate between Gods and men		
		Stella	16	Fuoco: intermediate between mundane and celestial things		
		Luna	17	Stelle		
		Sole	18	Luna		
		Angelo: the intelligence governing the planets and the stars	19	Sole		
		Giustizia: God, the first Mover	20	Mondo: the world cannot be without religion, represented by the four Evangelists		
		Mondo: includes everything and this game as well, which is a portrait of man who is himself a micro-world	21	Agnolo: the Celestial Paradise where blessed souls triumph		
				Bastoni: ancient wars	The four suits	
				Spade: modern wars		
				Coppe: during peace men are happy and wine makes men happy		
				Danari: also money makes men happy		
				Perfection of number Four (Ficino)		

DISCORSO DIL S.
FRAN. PISCINA
DA CARMAGNVOLA
SOPRA L'ORDINE
DELLE FIGVRE
de Tarocchi.

Dedicato al Ill. S. Rettor del Studio del
Serenissimo Duca di Sauoia.

IN MONTE REGALE
Appresso Lionardo Torrentino.
M D LXV.

A short introduction to Francesco Piscina's *Discorso*

Francesco Piscina's moralization of the Tarot, here translated for the first time, may be the earliest ever attempted. It is very likely, however, that he wrote within no more than a few years of the second, undated and anonymous, *Discorso* in this volume. Nevertheless, he alludes to other opinions on the subject (e.g. p. 13, concerning the placement of the Fool), indicating that the subject was a matter of discussion before his work appeared, while insisting that his is the only valid one (p. 29).

Piscina explained that he "composed this work ... because of a sudden caprice that entered our mind during a feast day, upon seeing a very honoured and gentle Lady of this city pleasantly playing..." The source of his inspiration prefigures that of Antoine Court (de Gébelin), the author of a much more influential moralization of the Tarot over two centuries later, who, upon seeing some ladies playing the game of Tarot, was immediately inspired to explain the meaning of the figures and their sequence. While the basis of Piscina's and Court's explanations are very different, both are attempts to provide a coherent explanation, in the context of a moral narrative, for the imagery and the sequence of the Tarot pack each encountered that day.

For Piscina, the "good order" of the subjects of the 22 trumps is proof that the inventor was "a good and loyal follower of the Catholic and Christian faith". He shows by their order how a lower card is subject to a higher, how everything below Fortune is subject "to the insolence of Fortune", and how everything below the Death card is appropriately subject to Death, but that, in the sequence of the cards, "there follows nothing on which it has any power." He considers that Temperance, following Death, "can here be interpreted as any other virtue, that does not fear the strikes of Death", while the remainder of the sequence is a gradual ascent from "earthly things" to the highest "celestial things", including the World, with religion (shown by the four Evangelists) as its guiding principle, and "the image of Paradise", depicted with an Angel "singing and playing". After this, Piscina discusses the "perfect" number four, and sees the four suits as "four qualities of things", adding that they represent "the diversity of the conditions of human life", such as Batons and Swords for times of war, and Cups and Coins for the peaceful life.

Piscina's Tarot trumps seem to resemble and largely follow a sequence in a group that Michael Dummett christened "C", and Tom Tadfor Little labelled "Western".[1] This group includes the game and the style of cards found in Lombardy, Piedmont/Savoy, France and the rest of Europe outside of Italy. The C group characteristically places Temperance immediately after Death, and has the World as the highest card. But Piscina's descriptions also indicate that the game of Tarot he knew had peculiar features not present in any other game of the Western family, features that are found elsewhere only in Bologna. In particular, the presence of two Popes and two Emperors, which are played as equal cards (p. 17), and the placement of the "Agnolo" (Angel) higher than the World card (p. 25). Since these features were traditional in Piedmontese and Savoyard games as they are known from descriptions beginning in the 18th century, Dummett proposed that the regional game was introduced directly from Bologna at an early time, although the only style of cards known to have been used in Piedmont and Savoy has always been of the C or Western type instead of the Bolognese pack. How and when these features entered the Piedmontese game remains one of the unresolved problems in playing-card history.[2]

We know of only two copies of the *Discorso*, one in the Biblioteca pubblica e Casa della cultura (Public Library and Arts Centre) Fondazione Achille Marazza in Borgomanero (Piedmont, Italy), and another in a private collection (Piscina/Berti 1995). We believe that this 1565 edition is the only one, but some Italian book catalogues, like the online EDIT 16 (http://edit16.iccu.sbn.it) and the catalogue of 16th-century Piedmontese books, *Le cinquecentine piemontesi*,[3] mention another edition, of 1570, differently titled "Della significatione delle figure de i tarocchi. | Nel Monteregale, 1570.", for which, however, they offer no other evidence than authors of the 17th (Rossotto, 1667), 18th (Derossi, 1784) or early 19th century (Grassi, 1804) all relying upon their predecessors. No actual copy has ever been recorded. It is highly probable that this 1570 'ghost' edition was mixed up with Piscina's other book, *An statuta feminarum exclusiua porrigantur ad bona forensia*, Monteregali, 1570.

Of Francesco – or Giovanni Francesco – Piscina we know little. Nicola

---

1 For the three types of the Tarot trump orders, see Dummett 1980, pp. 387-417. Little's descriptive and useful taxonomy can be found on his website (Little 1999).

2 Michael Dummett, "Unsolved Problems concerning Tarot and Italian Cards", posted on the IPCS website, 10 February 1999 (http://i-p-c-s.org/problis1.html), accessed 15/01/2010.

3 *Le cinquecentine piemontesi*, Marina Bersano Begey and Giuseppe Dondi ed., v. II, Turin, 1966, n° 1126.

Ghietti[4] states that "we have many accounts [!] of his life" and informs us that Piscina was born "intorno al 1540" to "the famous captain Gian Giacomo who, distinguishing himself during the battle of Ceresole [1544] between the Imperial army and the French, was granted the honour of adding France's fleur-de-lis to his coat-of-arms by King Francis I." Whether this is true or not, we cannot say for Ghietti does not quote any reference.

It seems Francesco Piscina was indeed born into a prominent family of Carmagnola, near Turin, then belonging to the Marquisate of Saluzzo, a French fief. According to Nicola Ghietti again, he married Leonora, daughter of Francesco Saluzzo of Bonavalle, and graduated in "both laws" (Roman and Canon) at the University of Monte Regale, today's Mondovì, which had recently been established by Duke Emanuele Filiberto of Savoy in 1560 (and was moved to Turin in 1566). He had been there a student of Giacomo Menochio (1532-1607)[5] who held the chair of Canon Law from 1561 to 1565.

It is hard to believe it was with this light-hearted Italian discourse on Tarot that Piscina got a doctorate, and it is much safer to place his final graduation in 1566, when the Mondovì University closed its doors and was moved to Turin. The book *Disputatio Francisci Piscinae iureconsulti Carmagnolien. An statuta feminarum exclusiua porrigantur ad bona forensia,* Monteregali : [Tipografia Torrentiniana] : sumptibus Francisci Dulcij, & Bartholomaei Galli, 1570, is more likely to have been his doctoral dissertation.

Ghietti also tells us that by 1571 Francesco Piscina was a judge in Savigliano (western Piedmont) and that he was knighted in 1575, then moved with his family to Saluzzo in 1580.[6] After this date we hear nothing more of Francesco Piscina,[7] but his son Giovanni Giacomo (or Gian Giacomo, Gianjacopo), who became a lawyer too, rose to prominence, being a prefect in Piedmont in 1607-9, then a senator (1610), and a diplomat in the Duke of Savoy's service. In 1623, he was elected President of the Senate of Piedmont, and two years later he was appointed as Grand Chancellor of the Duchy. He was made a Count in 1630, and died in 1651.

4 In Piscina/Berti 1995, p. 3 'Prefazione'.

5 On Menochio, see Cesare Beretta, "Jacopo Menochio giurista e politico", *Bollettino della Società Pavese di Storia Patria,* XCI (1991), pp. 245-77.

6 Notices on Francesco Piscina can be found in: *Piemontesi illustri,* IV, Turin, 1784, p. 100; Onorato Derossi, *Scrittori piemontesi, savoiardi, nizzardi registrati nei cataloghi del vescovo Francesco Agostino Della Chiesa e del monaco Andrea Rossotto,* Turin, 1790, pp. 41-2; Goffredo Casalis, *Dizionario geografico-storico-statistico-commerciale...,* III, Turin, 1836, s.v. 'Carmagnola'; Carlo Dionisotti, *Storia della magistratura piemontese,* 2 vols., Turin, 1881, II, Appendice, Biografie.

7 A few authors cite a text called *Consigli di Francesco Piscina,* published in Venice in 1591, but it is untraceable in any of the catalogues available to us.

DISCORSO DIL S.
FRAN. PISCINA
DA CARMAGNVOLA
SOPRA L'ORDINE

DELLE FIGVRE

de Tarocchi.

Dedicato al Ill. S. Rettor del Studio del
Serenissimo Duca di Savoia.

IN MONTE REGALE

Appresso Lionardo Torrentino.

M D LXV.

AL ILLUSTRE S. RINALDO Ressano da Pinarolo Rettor dignissimo del studio di sua Altezza, Francesco Piscina.

Posciachè quando V.S. fu fatto nostro Rettore per crudel mia sorte, la qual giamai non m'abbandonò, ne pur adesso lascia di tormentarmi, in varie maniere, non mi fu concesso si come haveva ordinato, monstrarle, parte del-l'affettione & devotione ch'io gl'havea & ho con una oratione pubblicamente lodando le infinite e bellissime virtù soe, le quali da essa sempre ben adoperate & ispetialmente in questa diffesa della dignità soa, saranno bastanti a renderla immortale; la onde pubblicando io questo mio rozzo discorso a richiesta de gl'Illustri Signori Daniele Malabaila e Francesco Belli, e d'altri miei amici e padroni a' quali non ho voluto né possuto oppormi e particolarmente a questi due Nobilissimi e Valorosi Cavaglieri, l'ho voluto dedicar qual egli si sia a V.S. pregandola che con amorevol faccia lo vogli accettare, che oltre che farà cosa degna dell'humanità sua, darà etiamdio animo a qualche gentile spirito e pellegrino ingegno di ragionevolmente magnificarla descrivendo questo suo viaggio fatto alla Corte del Serenissimo Principe tanto ad essa honorato, quanto all'Università degli Scuolari utile, col che facendo fine poiché gl'havro basciato le generose e liberalissime mani prego N.S. Dio per compimento d'ogni sua felicità. Data nella famosa Accademia di Monte Regale il Celebratissimo giorno della festa del Spirito Santo M D LX V.

DISCOURSE OF Mr.
FRANCESCO PISCINA
OF CARMAGNOLA
ON THE ORDER
OF THE FIGURES
of Tarot.
Dedicated to the Illustrious Rector of the College of
the Most Serene Duke of Savoy.[1]

IN MONTE REGALE,[2]
by Lionardo Torrentino,
1565.

To the Illustrious Mr. Rinaldo Ressano from Pinerolo,[3] most worthy Rector of the College of his Highness - *Francesco Piscina*.

When you, my lord, were made our Rector, my cruel fortune, that never parted from me, and also now keeps tormenting me in various ways, did not allow me to show to you a part of the affection & devotion that I had & have for you with a public speech in which I would have praised your infinite and most beautiful virtues, which, since you have always used them for the best & in particular in this defence of your own dignity, will be enough to make you immortal. Publishing this rough discourse, as requested by the Illustrious Lords Daniele Malabaila[4] and Francesco Belli,[5] and others of my friends and masters to whom I could not oppose myself, and in particular to these two very noble and valiant knights, I wanted to dedicate it, whatever its value, to you, my lord. I pray you to accept it with a benevolent face: doing so, you will do something that is worthy of your humanity, and will also give courage to some kind spirit and wandering intelligence to praise you with reason, describing your travel to the Court of the Most Serene Prince where you have been so much honoured, and that has been so useful to the university of the scholars. With this I finish, after having kissed your very generous and liberal hands, praying Our Lord God to accomplish all your happiness. Given in the famous Academy of Monte Regale in the much Celebrated Holy Day of the Holy Spirit 1565.

RAGIONAMENTO
DIL S. FRAN. PISCINA
DA CARMAGNVOLA
SCVOLAR DI LEGGI
FATTO SOPRA
l'ordine
DELLE FIGVRE
DE TAROCCHI.

Havendo io Honorati Lettori brevemente a favellare del ordine delle figure de tarocchi, non voglio per hora altamente distendermi in dimostrare,
quanto eccellente e divina cosa sia l'Ordine in questo Universo, perciochè chi
non sa che dove non è ordine, ivi è confusione? E dove questa è nulla di
buono si può fare, e perché ciò insegna l'esperienza Maestra delle cose, però
non mi sforzerò altrimente artificiosamente monstarlo, considerando
adunque il giuditioso Autore di questo giuoco di quanto momento fia il
buon'ordine, e si come non basta all'Oratore per conseguir il fine appostosi
di persuadere havere ingegnosamente trovato & giuditiosamente eletto quello che ha da dire, & al Capitano dell'esercito non basta per acquistar la
desiderata vittoria, l'haver trovato e scielto soldati a piede & a cavallo, l'ar-
tiglierie & altre cose necessarie, se quelle non sono da lui con buon ordine
disposte & adoperate, secondo che richieggono l'occasioni così che poco
diletto havrebbeno apportato queste soe figure, se in disporle non havesse
seguito & usato, un bel ordine si come si conviene: perciò egli non ha man-
cato d'ogni diligenza in così fare.
   Ma venendo hormai all'intento nostro dico, che fu opinione & ancor
hoggi è appresso del volgo il piu delle volte sciocco e inconsidreato, che il
pazzo qui nel ordine de Tarocchi, sia stato posto il primo nel ordine, per-
suadendosi che l'Autore & Inventore habbi voluto rappresentare qualche
favola, o dirò così (impropriamente parlando) Comedia, & venir fuori il
Matto primo per esser costume in questi così fatti solazzi e rappresentationi,
che uscisca fuori prima de gl'altri alcuno in abito strano, piacevole, e che
muova gl'huomini a riso come è solito de Buffoni, Pazzi, e d'altre di così fatta
maniera persone. Ma grandemente costor fallono, la onde noi più sottilmente
considerando la mente del'Inventore diciamo egli haver voluto in queste soe
figure dimonstrare, molti Morali amaestramenti, e sotto qualche difficoltà
morder i cativi e pestiferi costumi, & insegnare quante Attioni hoggidi fuori
del diritto & honesto governate, & al contrario del dovere, e giusto maneg-
giate siano, per il che evidentemente non solo hà dimonstrato essere Buono e
fedel seguace della Catholica e Cristiana fede, ma etiamdio molto esperto &

DISCOURSE
OF Mr. FRANCESCO PISCINA
OF CARMAGNOLA,
STUDENT OF LAWS,

MADE UPON

the order

OF THE FIGURES

OF TAROT.

Honoured readers, since I must briefly reason about the order of the figures of Tarot, I do not want now to discuss in length the high demonstration of how this Universe is an excellent and divine thing, because who does not know that where there is no order there is confusion? And where there is confusion, nothing good can be done, as is taught by experience, teacher of all things, therefore, I will not try to prove this with more art. So the wise author of this game considered the importance of good order. For an orator, to reach his goal of persuading, it is not enough to have ingeniously found & wisely chosen what he has to say. For the captain of an army, it is not enough, in order to obtain the desired victory, to have found and chosen infantry soldiers and cavalry, artillery and other necessary things, if those are not deployed and used with a good order, according to the situation. So these figures would have given but little pleasure if he had not placed them following & using a beautiful and convenient order. He applied all diligence in doing so.

But now, coming to our subject, I say that the opinion of the foolish and unreasonable masses has been, and still is today, that the fool has been placed as the first in the order of Tarot because the author and inventor wanted to represent a fable or (improperly said) a comedy: the Fool comes out first because it is common, in such amusing shows, that the first to appear is someone who wears a strange and pleasant costume, making people laugh, as usually the Jokers and the Fools and similar people do. But those people are grossly wrong. With more subtle consideration of the mind of the inventor, we say that he wanted to illustrate with his figures many moral teachings, and under some difficulty, to bite into bad and dangerous customs, & show how today many actions are done without goodness and honesty, and are accomplished in ways that are contrary to duty and rightfulness. In this way he proved to be not only a good and loyal follower of the Catholic and Christian faith, but also a true expert and excellent in the customs of civil

eccellente de ì costumi della vita Civile. Poscia che di ventidoe figure che ha posto & eletto non vi ne sia pur una che ben ponderata non apporti seco grandissima e profondissima consideratione & che non sij degna d'essere benissimo osservata. La ragione dunque perche il matto sia il primo ella puo esser questa per voler significare il principio & il fine della vita del huomo: cioè la fanciullezza, e la vecchiezza. Nella quale età par à certo modo che gl'huomini siano pazzi poi che sono privi di senno & intelletto. E perciò il pazzo è posto il primo a questo intento. Ma questa se ben è piena di grande consideratione, un'altra nondimeno se ben parra da burla non voglio lasciare, ne meno tacere. Ad intelligenza della quale, per maggior chiarezza è da sapere, quel che si legge in una molto piacevole & arguta Comedia finta da ì dottissimi Intronati, famosissimi Accademici di Siena, non senza grave giuditio in una dilettevole controversia che fra due Avarissimi Hosti. Segue che tutti gl'huomini di qualunque sorte si voglia, accadendogli d'ir in viaggio solevano alloggiar prima alla hosteria dello Specchio; ma da molto tempo in qua andarsene tutti più volentieri à quella dil Matto, si come più convenevole, al volere, & alle attioni loro. E perciò non senza grandissimo mistero vegiamo il Pazzo nel giuoco de Tarocchi esser dipinto à modo che sguardi indietro ad uno specchio, beffandosi della fama dello specchio perduta appresso tutti gl'huomini, ì quali solevano concorrere all'hosteria soa; e perciò in faccia molto gioiosa si rallegra, anzi si gloria del credito ch'egli ha, si che tutti gli huomini gli corrono dietro, e lo segue colui che che s'addomanda il Bagato in habito di hoste, non senza accorto avedimento, percioche si come le Insegne delle Hostarie sono più presto da Forastieri vedute che cercano d'allogiare che gl'istessi hosti, & che e[t]iamdio l'insegne sogliano dar buon credito all'hostarie come veggiamo, in quelle de Gigli, Aquile, Falconi, Corone e Re, le quali in tutte le buone e famose città demonstrano buon allogiamento, così il Matto è stato anteposto come figura dell'hosteria al Bagato che è l'Hoste, per significar ella esser quella famosa Hosteria nella qual la magior parte de gli huomini sogliano andar ad allogiare.

Ne qui tacero io perche tanto da Giuocatori il Matto sii desiderato, peroche oltre che egli è molto buono & utilissimo, nelle Brezicole. Avvengha che supplisca al Re, & alla Regina significati per ì gran Signori e Prencipi à Cavaglieri intesi per gli huomini di mediocre stato, & al Fante interpretato per il restante dell'humana generatione se alcun di costoro mancasse, non altro volendoci denotare senon che la maggior parte di questa sorte di gente, hà non so che di parentado e domestichezza col Matto, come colui che intervenghi per loro ad ogni sua absenza è nondimeno etiamdio evidente e manifesto argomento della gran pazzia de giuocatori, ì quali secondo il comun proverbio appetiscano volentieri i simili à loro, e che è di pazzia segno più

life: because in the twenty two figures he has placed and chosen, there is none that, being pondered with attention, does not bring with itself the greatest and deepest meaning & that is not worthy to be examined in detail. So the reason why the fool is the first could be to mean the beginning and the end of human life, i.e. childhood and old age. In that age it somehow seems that people are fools, because they have no wisdom or intelligence, and the Fool is placed as the first for this reason. This [explanation] is full of great consideration, but I do not want to leave out unmentioned another one, even if it will seem to be a joke. In order to make it clear, you must know that it can be read, in a very pleasant and acute comedy written by the very learned Intronati,[6] of the famous Academy in Siena, not devoid of seriousness, of the amusing controversy between two very tight-fisted innkeepers: all people of any kind, when they had to travel, used to go to the Inn of the Mirror, but for a long time they had preferred to go to that of the Fool, more appropriate to their will and their actions. This is why, with great mystery, we see the Fool in the game of Tarot being represented in such a way that he looks behind towards a mirror, making fun of the fame of the Mirror, that is lost among all people, who once used to go to that inn. This is why his face is so joyful, he rejoices and glories in the credit he receives, so that all men run behind him. He is followed by the one that is called the Bagat, dressed as an innkeeper, not without subtlety, because as the signs of the Inns are seen by travellers in search of lodging before they see the innkeepers, and as the signs used to give good credit to the inns, as we see in those of the Lilies, Eagles, Falcons, Crowns and Kings, that in all good and famous cities show good lodging, in the same way the Fool, being the figure of the inn, has been put before the Bagat, who is the Innkeeper, meaning that famous inn to which most people used to go.

I will also say why the Fool is so much desired by Players, because not only it is very good and useful, in the combinations it can take the place of the King and the Queen, meaning the great Lords and Princes, of Knights, meaning men of average condition, of the Page, interpreted as the rest of human generation, if any of them is missing:[7] this wants to represent that most of this sort of people has some kind of closeness and familiarity with the Fool, being the one that replaces them when they are absent. This is also a clear and explicit argument of the great madness of players, who according to the well-known proverb, are willing to desire those that are similar to themselves. What is a clearer sign of madness than wanting to put under the dominion of fortune what they are securely holding in their hands, almost with the cer-

espresso che voler porre quel che essi hanno sicuro in mano in arbitrio della
fortuna & à sicuro quasi pericolo di perderlo? è perciò si come sicuramente
sappiamo pochi ò nessuno de pazzi fornir la lor vita in buono & honorato
fine, così giornalmente habbiamo non rari essempi di giuocatori, ì quali
poche volte ò non mai consegnano util fine delle lor'attioni, per il che si può
comprendere quanto ben sia l'astenersi dal giuoco, il quale spesse fiate è
causa della perdita non de ì danari solamente ma etiamdio della vita, e molte
volte del anima istessa.

Ma lasciati questi ragionamenti (i quali però alcune volte mi converrà
seguire distendendomi à discorrere fuori del suggetto) descendiamo la onde
ci dipartimmo, è seguano nel ordine delle figure doppo il pazzo & il Bagato
Imperatori e Papi intesi per ì gran Prencipi non ch'essi siano pazzi e matti, &
allogiar vadino al Hosteria di questa insegna, ma per monstrare quel che è
cioè che à Principi molto dilettano i Buffoni & altri simili a questi, e questo
forza è quasi che faciano per ricrear gli spiriti loro travagliati da continoe fat-
tiche e fastidij mentali che da ogni hora gli sopravengono.

Non è adesso maraviglia che giuocando l'Imperatore di minor dignità &
authorità de ì Papi alcune volte gli vinca è pigli, percioche questo altro (al
mio parere) l'Inventore significar non ha volutto se non che si come nell'His-
torie antiche e moderne leggiamo spesso accada che gl'Imperatori vincano e
faciano prigioni i Papi, alcune volte per colpa e legitime cause che a ciò fare
questi spingano, come di Bonifacio ottavo è scritto, altre fiate per avaritia &
insolenza de Capitani di quelli, si come quasi à nostri tempi è avvenuto al
Beatissimo Clemente Settimo, la cui dignità insieme con gl'infelici Cardinali
& il resto de Santissimi sacerdoti fu crudelmente manomessa dalla fier ingor-
digia, & insatiabil desiderio d'oro da gli Barbari soldati, del Augustissimo &
Invittissimo Imperator Carlo Quinto, e questi due essempi bastino per hora:
in ordine delle figure viene appresso costoro il ritratto di Cupido da i super-
stitiosi Antichi chiamato il Dio d'Amore, il quale doppiamente, e in due fog-
gie può pigliarsi, e prima per Amor significando quella pazzia che generata
ne i cuor de gli huomini gli fa arrabbiare, ma spetialmente secondo l'opinion
de dotti, nelle persone otiose e involte in ogni delicatezza, e perciò sii stato
posto amor doppo questi gran Prencipi, come coloro che fiano più dati alle
delitie de gl'altri huomini, o veramente diremo, che l'habbi l'Inventor posto
(e forse più certamente) per affettione e passione, e perciò seguiti la Giustitia
così immediatamente dopo questi Prencipi per esser propriamente di loro
l'administrar e governar la Giustitia, & che la Giustitia vinca le passioni, e
non si lasci da esse signoreggiare, come che ella sii salda e perfettamente secondo la diffinitione d'Aristotile, & che habbi da esser retta e maneggiata
senza passione & affetto. Ma perché Amor è qui dipinto in forma di quel vol-

tainty of losing it? As we surely know that few or none of the fools finished his life in a good and honourable way, so we daily have many examples of players, who seldom or never reach good results with their actions: so we can understand how it is good to abstain from play, which often is the cause of losing not only one's money, but also life and many times the soul itself.

But leaving these considerations (to which I will from time to time go back, digressing from the subject) we now go down to where we started from. In the order of the figures, after the Fool and the Bagat, there follow Emperors and Popes, representing high Princes. Not that they are crazy and foolish, and go lodging in the Inn with that sign, but showing what is, i.e. that Princes take much pleasure in Jokers and the like: and they are almost obliged to do so, in order to refresh their spirit, troubled by the continuous fatigue and mental worries that come to them at any time.

Now you do not have to be surprised that when playing the Emperor, of a lesser authority and dignity than the Popes, sometimes he wins and takes them:[8] in my opinion, the inventor wanted to signify that, as we can read in ancient and modern histories, it often happens that the Emperors win and imprison the Popes, sometimes for fault and rightful causes that push them to do so, as it is written about Boniface VIII, other times for greed and insolence of their captains, as almost at our times happened to the Blessed Clement VII, whose dignity, together with the unhappy cardinals and the rest of the holy priests was cruelly offended by the fierce greed and unlimited desire of gold of the barbarous soldiers of the very august and undefeated Emperor Charles V.[9] Let these two examples be enough, for the time being. In the order of the figures, after them comes the portrait of Cupid, that the superstitious ancients called the god of Love, which can be interpreted in two ways. The first is that Love means that craziness that, when generated in the hearts of men, makes them lose their reason, in particular, according to the learned, in idle people that are involved in any kind of delight, so love has been put after those high Princes, as they are more keen to pleasure than other men. Or we can truly say (maybe with greater certainty) that the inventor has placed it to represent affection and passion, and so Justice follows so immediately after these Princes because it belongs to them to administer and rule Justice, & that Justice wins passions, and must not be ruled by them, and that it must be firm, and perfectly in accordance with Aristotle's definition,[10] and it has to be right and handled without passion & affection. But Love is here represented in the form of the vulgar one that deprives us of our intellect and judgement, and takes away any good mind, in brief as an imperfect thing, and so less

gare che ci ruba l'intelletto, & il giuditio, e che ne rapisce ogni buona mente, e finalmente per cosa imperfetta, e perciò men degna anzi contraria alla Giustitia secondo la diffinitione d'essa sopra addutta, d'Aristotile, che perciò Amore sii inferiore alla Giustitia, & che essa lo superi, & in maggior grado d'esso posta sia, ma questo se ben par che alquanto repugni a quella dichiaratione non però la vogliamo lasciare come più morale il che con questa nova ragione confermo, ch'essendo la Giustitia per iniquità de molti cativi Magistrati tratti da qualche grand'utile assai fiate non sii governata, con passioni & affetti, ma che però questo sii malamente fatto, & ch'ella venghi e debba esser giustamente maneggiata, & con constante, perpetua & immutabile voluntà, secondo la diffinitione de Giureconsulti et etiamdio habbi da superar ogni appetito, che perciò la Giustitia, vinca, superi, & signoreggi, l'Amore, che gl'huomini fuori della via della ragione molte volte fa trasportare, quanto all'esser egli qui dipinto, in forma di quel volgare, diciamo questo poter esser stato, fatto per che l'Affetto non si poteva forse in altra più accomodata forma figurare, che nel imagine di Cupido, conciosiache etiamdio che l'amor volgare altro non è secondo i Platonici che un Appetito sfrenato, & poche volte non ragionevol desiderio di conseguir alcuna cosa, alla qual s'habbi posto affettione.

Ora dietro alla figura della Giustitia viene il Carro Triomphante, nell'Ottavo numero e nel Nono la Fortezza lo segue, con la Fortuna, nel Decimo grado collocata, ì quali tre ritratti sono con bellissimo ordine qui posti à Papi, Imperatori & Prencipi referendoci, come coloro il cui proprio sia triomphare delle loro magnanime imprese, e vittoriose fattioni, e quanto alla Fortezza appertiene avengha che questi Gran Prencipi siano più forti di tutti gli altri huomini puolsi anco dir questa insegna della Fortezza esser posta per causa della Giustitia, dandoci ad intendere (quel che certamente spesse volte avviene) non rare volte usarsi forza alla Giustitia, le spetie della quale si pono diversamente pigliare. O veramente altrimenti parlando che essendo la Giustitia da se stessa debile ch'abbi bisogno di Fortezza ad esser secondo le leggi e constitutioni governata, onde più e più fiate vegiamo i prudenti Magistrati ne i gran pericoli e questioni alle quali non basta la Forza de i birri & altri sergenti a ciò deputati chiamar forte soccorso & agiuto a sufficienza per diffesa della Giustitia aciochè ella (secondo le constitutioni delle divine & humane leggi) non sii violata.

Ma finalmente nel Decimo Grado è posta l'effigie della Fortuna, volendo (cred'io) l'Autore significare che benchè grandi, forti e potenti siano Papi & Imperatori, questi nondimeno lor honori, triomphi, potentati, e grandezze & universalmente parlando queste tutte terrene cose & ogn'altro temporal bene esser soggetto all'insolente Fortuna, onde non meno prudentemente che leg-

worthy of or contrary to Justice according the above mentioned definition by Aristotle, this is why Love is inferior to Justice and he is won by her, and she is put in a higher place than he is. But I do not want to leave this behind because it is more moral, even if it seems to be in conflict with that statement, so I confirm [the above argument] with this new reason: it happens that the iniquity of many bad magistrates, attracted by some great gain, makes them administer Justice in accordance with their own passions and affections, but this is badly done, because Justice must be rightly administered, with a constant, perpetual and immutable will, according to the definition of Jurisprudence, and it must win all appetites. Since Justice wins, surpasses & governs Love, that often takes men out of the way of reason, we say that here it is painted in its vulgar form because affection perhaps could not be represented in any better way than in the image of Cupid, because, according to the Platonists, vulgar love is but an unbounded appetite,[11] and sometimes an unreasonable desire to obtain something for which we have affection.

Now, after the figure of Justice, we find the Triumphant Chariot, in the eighth number, in the ninth it is followed by Strength, with Fortune placed in the tenth position. Those three portraits are put here with the most beautiful order, making reference to the Popes, Emperors & Princes, as those for whom it is appropriate to triumph from their great enterprises, and victorious wars; for what belongs to Strength, it happens that these great Princes are stronger than all other men. One can also say that this symbol of Strength is placed here because of Justice, telling us (and certainly this often happens) that it is not unusual that Justice is forced, the types of which can be taken in different ways. Or truly, speaking differently, Justice, being weak on its own, needs Strength to be ruled according to laws and constitutions: so we often see that the prudent magistrates, when there is a great danger or there are questions for which the police and other officials that manage such affairs are not enough, strongly ask for help in defence of Justice so that it is not violated, according to the constitutions of divine and human laws.

Finally in the tenth place the image of Fortune is placed: I believe that the author meant that, although Popes and Emperors are great, strong and powerful, their honours, triumphs, powers and greatness, and in general all these earthly things and any other temporal good, are subject to the insolence of Fortune. So what Ariosto has written in his third Canto is no less prudent than elegant:

Fortune gives and takes everything;
only on virtue it has no power[12]

giadramente ha lasciato nel terzo Canto l'Ariosto scritto:
   Che dona e tole ogni altro ben Fortuna
   Sol in virtù non ha possanza alcuna
   E perciò la Fortuna è posta in più eminente luogo e grado di tutte quel'altre nominate cose, come che tutte le domini signoreggi & a suo modo volga,
ma forsi potrami alcun domandare, perché la Giustitia che è virtù honoratissima sia sottoposta all'inconstanza della Fortuna, e rispondendo dico lasciando molte altre solutioni, ch'io potrei addurre ma forse troppo odiose e
pericolose. Che essendo la Giustitia anch'ella cosa caduca e transibile (parlando però sanamente di questa terrena) che perciò sii sotto il regimento e
maneggio della Fortuna, o veramente conciò sia che la Fortuna sii instabile,
& che hora rubi hora doni & che la Giustitia sii hora da uno governata, hora
da un altro che per questa ragione l'Autore l'habbi posta fra quelle cose che
la Fortuna regge e governa.
   Il Vecchio Gobbo vien poi carco d'affanni e pensieri che vince e supera la
Fortuna, il qual ci vol significar un prudente conseglio, col qual si vince ogni
Fortuna, perciò che nelle cose prospere non c'induce punto a gloria ne a
superbia ne meno nell'averse e poco seconde ci lascia disperare. Il che affer-
miamo e confirmiamo con questa ragione non del tutto degna d'esser
rimossa. Conciosiachè un saggio e prudente superi il suo Fato e Destino, che
par non so che più d'humano, quanto maggiormente signoreggia e sarra
vincitore della Fortuna, la quale è terrena, e per nulla quasi da prudenti ripu-
tata, il Vecchio dico è posto per un considerato conseglio & ottimo giuditio,
avvengha che sia proprio degl'huomini invecchiati e maturi il consigliar bene.
Posciachè accada che quel ch'essi dicono l'abino più volte per isperienza
provato. Qui sovviemmi d'un detto che parmi haver udito dall'eccellentissi-
mo e maraviglioso in ogni maniera di scienze il Signor Giovan Battista
Giraldi mio precettore nella Tragica facondia un altro Sofocle e non meno di
bellissimi e profondissimi concetti ripieno che nel esporgli nell'una e nell'altra lingua eloquentissimo: che chi vuol ben operare una facenda la faci due
volte, ma perché questo non sempre ne tutti puono fare essequiscala secondo
il conseglio e parere de gl'homini vecchi e maturi, i quali per la lunghezza de
gl'anni di rado avviene che non l'habbino havuta in esperimento & a prova.
   Questo Vecchio segue l'Impiccato giunto a questo punto per haver sprez-
zato il buon conseglio. Il qual l'Iventor ha posto per rappresentare un huomo
tristo, falso, vitioso, pestifero, e brevemente concludendo (poiché il buon
conseglio dipende dalle virtù) per un huomo privo a fatto d'ogni virtù che
senza consiglio come disperato s'è impicato, per dimonstrar & avisar il pes-
simo fine che fanno i speratori de i prudenti consegli, e per consequenza delle
virtù, la qual forte di gente per essere meritevolmente da ogniuno odiata

And this is why Fortune is put in a higher place and position than all the other things I have named: because she dominates and rules and turns in their own way all of them. Maybe someone will ask me why Justice, that is a very honoured virtue, is put under the inconstancy of Fortune: I will answer leaving out many other solutions that I could bring forth but that are possibly too hideous and dangerous. Justice is under the dominion and management of Fortune because it also is a perishable and transient thing (speaking strictly of the earthly one). Or maybe the author has put Justice among the things that are ruled and governed by Fortune because Fortune is not firm, now it steals and now it gives, & Justice is governed now by one, and now by someone else.

Then the Old Hunchback comes, charged with troubles and thoughts, and he wins and surpasses Fortune. He represents a prudent counsel, with which you can win any Fortune, because in prosperous things it does not make us proud or superb, and in adversities and unfavourable things it does not make us despair. This we affirm and confirm with the following reason, that does not deserve to be completely removed: a wise and prudent man wins over his Fate and Destiny, for [in him there is] something that is more than human, as much as he is a winner of Fortune, which is earthly and considered to be almost nothing by the prudent. I say the Old Man represents a well-pondered counsel and an excellent judgement: it happens that it belongs to old and mature men to give good advice, because it is the case that they have experienced many times whatever matter they talk about. Here I am reminded of something which I think I heard from Signor Giovan Battista Giraldi, a wonderful man who excels in all science, who was my teacher;[13] in the tragic art he is a second Sophocles, full of beautiful and deep concepts and perfectly eloquent in expressing them in both languages: if you want to do something well, do it twice. But since this cannot always be done by everybody, one should follow the advice and the opinion of old and mature men, who, for the length of their years, most of the time will have an experience with that thing.

The Old Man is followed by the Hanged Man, who came to this point because he despised all good advice. The inventor has placed him to represent a dishonest, false, vicious, pestiferous man: in order to conclude briefly (since good advice depends on virtues) a man completely devoid of any virtue, who hanged himself being as a desperate man without counsel. This shows the terrible end of those that despise prudent advice and, as a consequence, virtues: such people are rightly hated by everyone, and when they die they lose all their fame, and name, as if they were never been born. There

morendo perde dal tutto la soa fama, e nome come se giamai non fosse nata. E perciò segue la Morte che spenge del tutto la lor memoria, la qual Morte per esser estremo male, si come soleva dir Saffo poi che così havevano giudicato, i Dii non havendo voluto participarne, però va dietro a mali e a vitii, ben che si può dire e non senza qualche avveduta ragione che sia posta doppo tutte l'altre precedenti figure quivi la Morte per significarci che tutte quelle delle quali particolarmente di ciascuna habbiamo trattato siano soggette alla Morte. Come Papi, Imperatori, Triomphi, Fortezze, Vitii, e tutte l'altre sopranominate figure, e questo si verifica che doppo questa Morte nel Decimoterzo numero posta, non segue cosa sopra la quale ella habbi possanza alcuna.

La onde se ne viene la Temperanza che è virtù bellissima, poi che ci modera ne i piaceri corporali secondo che ordina la legge, e qui interpretata per ogn'altra virtù, la qual non teme punto colpo di Morte, ne meno inconstanza di Fortuna. Conciòsiachè anzi virtù siano quelle che rendono immortale e che secondo il parer dil Poeta traggono l'huomo dal sepolcro e lo serbano a longa & immortal vita.

Ma parendo ormai all'Autore d'haver posto imagini & essempi a bastanza di cose mortali e terrene, descende a por figure di cose più degne cioè celesti, ma per che secondo la dottrina de Filosofi la Natura non sopporta le mutationi troppo repentine, ne che si trapassi da l'un estremo all'altro senza debito mezo, perciò prima ch'ascendere alle cose celesti come termine estremo delle terrene pone essempi de Demoni, come che quasi essi se ben sono figliuoli de gli Dei come Melito interrogato da Socrate rispose così essere, non però sono veramente né terreni né celesti. Poscia che etiamdio è stato opinione di molti, & ispitialmente de Platonici, che siano i Demoni Spiriti che stanno fra l'Aria & che siano come certo mezo fra i Dii e gl'huomini.

Dietro i Demoni viene il Fuoco per debito mezo fra le stelle cose celesti, & le mondane per esser si come i Naturali o Filosofi affermano elemento che prima si trovi della Luna, Sole, e d'ogni altra Stella, ora havendo noi da entrare nelle cose celesti vedremmo l'Inventore haver osservato un bellissimo ordine, come che dii gran ornamento e splendore alle cose (si come nel principio di questo nostro Discorso habbiamo provato) pone adunque prima cose ch'appariscano la notte come ch'ella sii d'assai da meno dil giorno come adesso vi sarra manifesto cio è le stelle, che le notti serene veggiamo comparere & la Luna, la quale è vinta e superata dal Sole, e ciò per dimonstraci molte diverse e cose, fra quali per essempio e maggior chiarezza queste bastaranno, e prima volendo significare, di quanto maggior utile e dignità sia il giorno nel qual il Sol luce, della Notte, nella qual la Luna risplende, e etiamdio più degno il Sol della Luna, avvengha che ogni giorno faci il suo corso,

follows Death, that completely extinguishes any memory of them. As Sappho used to say, Death is the extreme evil, because the gods did not want to take any part in it:[14] this is why it follows the evils and the vices. But we can also say, not without some wise reason, that Death is placed here, after all the preceding figures, to mean all those of which we have discussed in detail are subject to Death, as Popes, Emperors, Triumphs, Strengths, Vices, and all the other above mentioned figures. And this is verified by the fact that after Death, placed in the thirteenth place, there follows nothing on which it has any power.

Then Temperance comes: a most beautiful virtue that moderates us in the pleasures of the body, according to the law, and that can here be interpreted as any other virtue, that does not fear the strikes of Death, nor the inconstancy of Fortune: on the contrary, virtues make men immortal, according to the opinion of the Poet, they take the man out of the grave and preserve him for a long and immortal life.[15]

Since the author thought to have put enough images and examples of mortal things, he moves to place figures of more worthy things, that is to say, celestial. But since nature does not allow changes that are too quick, nor that one moves from one extreme to the other without the due mean, before ascending to celestial things as the extreme end of earthly things he places examples of Demons: because, as Melito said answering Socrates' question,[16] they are sons of the gods but are neither earthly nor celestial. It has been the opinion of many, in particular the Platonists, that the Demons are spirits that are in the air & that they are somehow in the middle between gods and men.

After the Demons, comes Fire, as the due mean between the stars, which are celestial, and mundane things: it is, as affirmed by naturalists or philosophers, the element that is found before the Moon, the Sun and any other Star. Now, entering celestial things, we will see the most beautiful order followed by the inventor, giving things the greatest ornament and splendour (as we have proven at the beginning of this discourse). He places first those things that appear at night, since it is much less worthy than the day, as you will now see, i.e. the Stars, that appear in cloudless nights, and the Moon, which is won and surpassed by the Sun. In this way he shows many and diverse things among which for example (and for greater clarity they will be enough) firstly he represents that the day, when the Sun gives light, is of greater utility and dignity than the Night, when the Moon shines, and also that the Sun is more worthy than the Moon. It happens that the Sun makes his course every day, and that there cannot be a Day without the splendour

& che non possi star ne essere il Giorno senza splendore dil Sole, ma si ben la Notte senza il lume della Luna, con ciòsiachè la veggiamo alcune volte non comparere, se ben in tempo serenissimo. Per questa cagione ancor il Sol vince la Luna, come più utile d'essa all'humana generatione, ma finalmente concludendo si può dire, che il Sol sii maggior della Luna, e per ciò la vinca, per che egli è in più alto cielo situato della Luna, la qual affermano gl'Astrologi essere nel infimo cielo: ma il Sole, nel quarto. Il che perché è manifeste e chiaro ad ognuno, non dirò più oltre. Ma volendo finalmente l'Inventore con uno honorato e Cristiano fine fornir queste sue figure sotto le quali ha insegnato & accennato molti costumi, & amaestramenti Civili, ha posto per ultimo ritratto il Paradiso Celeste, nel qual Triomphano l'anime Beate, & vi ha fatto dipingere un Agnolo che cantando e sonando s'allegri di quelli Spiriti benedetti i quali la gratia d'Iddio prima e l'opere sue bone gl'hanno fatti degni di quella felicissima e sempiterna quiete: ma considerando egli che benchè la misericordia d'Iddio Ottimo e Grandissimo sii immensa, infinita & incomparabile, che nondimeno bisogna ben operare a conseguir la gloria del Paradiso, il che hanno insegnato i Santissimi Evangelisti, perciò ha prima dell'imagine del Paradiso fatto un ritratto d'essi quattro Evangelisti, intesi e significati pelle quattro insegne, Angelo, Bue, Aquila e Lione, le quali denotano quelli quattro Famosissimi e Sacrosanti Sostentacoli della soave & infallibil fede di Giesu Cristo, volendoci (come ho già detto) l'Inventor significare, che chi vorrà esser eletto d'Iddio, gli convien prima osservar i soi santissimi Comandamenti descritti da sopra nominati Beatissimi Scrittori, e così facendo saremo liberi dall'ingorde mani del rapacissimo Diavolo, il qual altro non studia che divorarci.

Hora, la figura del mondo in mezo questi quattro Santi Evangelisti l'Autore ha posto, per insegnarci che il mondo non può star senza religione i precetti, della quale hanno scritto questi Santissimi Evangelisti, essendo ella il principal fondamento della quiete e conservatione de stati e della felicità de popoli, e sanza la quale (si come già habbiamo in molti luoghi accennato) noi non potremmo salvar l'anima nostra, nata solo per servir al Grandissimo Signor Dio Nostro.

Ora se ben Honorati Lettori il principal intento nostro è stato di solamente favellare e discorrere sopra l'ordine delle figure de Tarocchi, non vogliamo però lasciar di ragionar alquanto sopra il restante delle carte del giuoco cose, però che apperterranno tutte alla materia nostra, la onde veggiamo l'Inventore haver posto di quattro qualità di cose, cioè Coppe, Danari, Spade e Bastoni, per significar (dicano molti ma senza però renderne fondamento alcuno) le quattro stagioni dell'anno, o veramente le quattro età dell'uomo, & altri le quattro parti del mondo, ma noi non così, ma dicciamo esser poste per la

of the Sun, but there can be a Night without the light of the Moon, because we see that sometimes it does not appear, even if the weather is perfectly clear. Moreover the Sun wins the Moon because it is more useful to human life. Finally, in conclusion, we can say that the Sun is more powerful than the Moon and wins on it because it is placed in an higher sky than the Moon, which according to the astrologers is in the lowest sky, while the Sun is in the fourth. This is perfectly clear to everybody, therefore I will add nothing more. Since the inventor wanted to conclude his figures, with which he has taught and illustrated many civil lessons, with an honoured and Christian purpose, he placed as last the image of Celestial Paradise, where blessed souls triumph. There he depicted an Angel that, singing and playing, rejoices in those blessed Spirits that were made worthy of that most happy eternal rest firstly by the Grace of God, and by their own good deeds. He considered that, although the mercy of our Good and Great God is immense, infinite & incomparable, nevertheless it is necessary to act well in order to gain the glory of Paradise, as taught by the Holy Evangelists. So, before the image of Paradise, he made a portrait of these four Evangelists, intended and signified by the four symbols, Angel, Ox, Eagle and Lion, who represent those four most famous and holy pillars of the sweet and infallible faith in Jesus Christ.[17] As I have already said, the inventor wanted to show that, whoever wants to be chosen by God, must first observe his holy Commandments described by the Blessed Writers I named above: in this way we will be free from the greedy hands of the rapacious Devil, whose only desire is to devour us.

Now, the author has placed the image of the world in the middle of these four Holy Evangelists, in order to teach us that the world cannot be without religion, whose precept has been written by these Holy Evangelists. Religion is the main foundation of the peace and conservation of the nations and of the happiness of the peoples: without it (as we have already said in many places) we could not save our soul, which was born only to serve the Greatest Lord Our God.

Now, most honoured readers, our main goal has been only to discuss about the order of the figures of Tarot. Yet we do not want to omit to reason about the rest of the cards of the game: all these things belong to our subject, because we see that the inventor has placed four qualities of things, that is Cups, Coins, Swords and Batons, to mean (as many say without giving any foundation) the four seasons of the year, or the four ages of man, and others the four parts of the world. On the contrary, we say they represent the diversity of the conditions of human life, i.e. war and peace, placing these for the

diversità e conditione del viver Humano ciò è guerra e pace, questi cioè ponendo per stagion di guerra, e quelli per il tempo della pace, per gli Bastoni rappresentando le antiche guerre, le quali con essi spesse fiate si terminorono non solamente nelle pubbliche fattioni, quanto ne i privati conflitti. Onde si legge che Caim uccise suo fratello Abel con un gran bastone che fu la prima guerra e discordia che fra gl'huomini fusse, eleggiamo etiamdio al tempo d'Alessandro Macedone esser state terminate discordie grandissime de potentissimi Stati con i soli Bastoni combattendo, per le Spade poi egli ha voluto dimonstrare le moderne guerre e Bataglie, le quali principalmente con esse soglian terminarsi, ma per le Coppe e Danari, ha voluto significar il moralissimo Inventore le conditioni de la pace, percioche essendo che al tempo d'essa gli huomini tutti vivano allegri, sicuri dalle crudeltà e travagli che seco apporta la guerra, ha poste le Coppe per il vino, che rende gl'huomini allegri & il cor loro lontano da ogni tristo e malenconico pensiero, ma etiamdio essendo che quasi ognuno nella pace vive contento, per ciò sono stati posti i danari per contentezza, conciosiache essi siano quelli che fanno gli uomini contenti, poscia che con essi noi possiamo adempier ogni nostro desiderio secondo il commune & usitato proverbio de Francesi, che con danari dicono potersi ogni cosa fare, benchè grande, difficile, e malagevole.

Ma non contenti noi di queste interpretationi un'altra vogliamo addurre non meno morale e quasi conforme a questa cio è avisando l'Inventor i Principi che nelle guerre significate per i Bastoni & le Spade, non vogliamo sempre usar le Spade, ma molte volte i Bastoni, i quali sono d'assai più leve castigho che le Spade, ma pur quando gl'inimici indiscreti & altri rei diventassero troppo insolenti, superbi, e licentiosi, per l'humanità de padroni, e Prencipi loro, allora, che s'habbino d'adoperar le spade, le quali puniscano con la morte la temerità e sceleragini loro, ma per che ogni cosa faciamo noi a qualche fine, & essendo il fine delle guerre la pace e tranquilità, nelle quali gl'huomini vivano allegri e molto contenti perciò ha posto il prudentissimo Autor nostro le Coppe e Danari, i quali come ho detto, rendano gl'huomini allegri e contenti: ora perchè più presto in numero quadernario che in altro potremo dire come in più perfetto anzi perfettissimo de gl'altri si come fra tutti & ispetialmente moderni il dottissimo Ficino ha scritto nel argomento fatto sopra il Timeo di Platone dal XX. Fino al 24. Cap.

Ma egl'è ormai tempo Amantissimi miei Lettori che ponendo io fine al trattar di questo soggetto, lasci occupar i vostri pellegrini & acutissimi ingegni ad altre facoltà che v'arrechino maggior utile di questo nostro discorso, il quale noi habbiamo composto più tosto per un subito cappriccio che ne viene nel capo un giorno di festa vedendo piacevolmente giuocar una Honoratissima e Gentilissima Gentildonna di questa Città, che di niuna

times of war and those for the times of peace. Batons represent ancient wars, which often were fought using them, not only in public wars but also in private conflicts. So we read that Cain killed his brother Abel with a large club, which was the first war and discord among men. We also read that, at the time of Alexander of Macedon, many great discords among powerful states were put to an end fighting only with clubs. With swords, he represented modern wars and battles, which are mainly fought using them. With Cups and Coins, the very moral inventor represented peaceful situations. Since in those times people live merrily, safe from the cruelty and troubles that war brings with itself, he placed the Cups to represent wine, which makes men merry & takes their heart away from any sad and melancholic thought. Since during peace almost everyone lives contentedly, Coins were added to represent contentment: because they make people content, since with them we can fulfil all of our desires, according to the well-known proverb of the French who say that with money it is possible to do anything, however great, difficult, and tiring.

But since we are not content with this interpretation, we want to add one more, that is not less moral and almost conforms to this one: the inventor advises the Princes that, in the wars which are represented by Batons and Swords, we do not want to always use the Swords, but many times the Batons, which are much lighter punishment than the Swords. But when arrogant enemies & other villains become too insolent, proud and impudent as a consequence of the humanity of their masters and Princes, then it is time to use Swords, in order to punish their temerity and their crimes with death. But since we do everything for some goal, and since the goal of wars is peace and tranquillity, so that men can live merry and content, our most prudent author has added Cups and Coins, that, as I said, make men merry and content. Now why in the number of four and not another we can say because it is more perfect than all the others. Among all, and especially modern writers, this has been explained by the very learned Ficino in his discussion on Plato's *Timaeus* from chapters XX to 24.[18]

But now it is time, my beloved readers, that I put an end to the discussion of this subject, leaving your wandering and very acute intellects to other occupations of more utility than our discourse. We have composed this work more because of a sudden caprice that came in our mind during a feast day, seeing a very honoured and gentle Lady of this city pleasantly playing, than for any hope of glory or any utility. On the contrary, we know perfectly that, seeing the title of the work, anyone may want to offer his own comments. But we were not deterred for this reason. If Christ, who could not fail in any

espettatione ne di gloria ne d'utile alcuno, anzi sappiamo di certissimo che visto il solo titolo dell'opera ognuno a suo modo vorrà cicalare, ma per ciò non ci siamo punto spaventati. Perciò che se Cristo il quale in niun modo poteva fallire, era delle buone e sante operationi biasimato perché non potrò io esser ripreso di cosa, nella quale so non esser gionto a segno di mediocre perfettione, questo sapevo io che molti diranno che un Taroccho ha favellato e trattato de Tarocchi, e se si può dire Tarocchamente. Ma dica pur ognun quel che vuole che nulla del loro cianciar mi curo: ohimè Dio egl'è pur la gran felicità de gl'huomini l'adempir le sue voglie, d'una cosa mi conforto e non poco mi consolo che a molti maligni miei Emuli dicendo mal di me sarra datto tanta fede come a me s'io li lodassi, e le lor opere insieme io volessi in quel buon conto & opinione havere, ch'essi credano che gl'huomini l'habino, ma grandemente costoro fallono, guardisi dunque ognuno a se stesso, e si ricordi di non avere tanto risguardo all'alitrui [sic] macchie, che non metta fantasia a i viti suoi, che oltre che saranno utile a loro, osservaranno etiamdio il divinissimo precetto dil Magno Iddio, il quale espressamente egl'ha comandato per bocca dil Redemtor nostro Giesu Cristo, il qual preghiamo che contenti ogn'uno, & spetialmente gl'honesti, casti e veri Amanti, come son'io, intendami chi po ch'i m'inte[n]d'io.

IL FINE

way, was blamed for his right and holy actions, why should not I be reproached for a thing in which I know I have not reached even the point of a mediocre perfection? I know that many will say that a Tarocco has *tarotly* (if I may say so) discussed and spoken of Tarot.[19] But anybody can say whatever they want: I do not care at all about their vain words. O, my God, after all to satisfy one's desires is the greatest happiness for men. I am somehow comforted and consoled by one thing: evil-minded imitators that may denigrate me will be as [little] believed as I would be were I to praise them and wished to hold their works in that high opinion that they believe they ought to be held. But they are grossly wrong. Let everyone look at himself, remembering not to give so much attention to other people's faults when he does not think about his own vices. Doing so will be useful to them, and they will also be in accordance to the divine precept of the Great God that was explicitly commended through the words of our Redeemer Jesus Christ, whom we pray to make everyone content, and in particular the honest, chaste and true lovers, as I am. Understand me who can, I know what I mean.

THE END

Notes and Comments to Piscina

1 Emanuele Filiberto (r. 1553-1580), the "second founder" of the Duchy, the ruler who introduced a tax on playing cards in his lands (see Depaulis 2005).

2 Now Mondovì, where Duke Emanuele Filiberto had established a short-lived university (1560-66).

3 Probably born around 1542/3, in Pinerolo, Rinaldo Ressano was for 1565-66 the rector (chosen among the students) of the University of Mondovì, from which he graduated as a lawyer in 1566 (Gioachino Grassi, *Dell'universita' degli studi in Mondovì*, Mondovì, 1804, p. 131). He seems to have also taken holy orders. After the move of the University to Turin he came back to Pinerolo. In Dec. 1567 a bull of Pope Pius V allowed him to quit the monk's habit, and in 1569 he is mentioned as Provost at Pinerolo; he must by then have become a canon. In 1578 he is styled Vicar-General for the St. Mary Abbey (Canon Alfredo Boiero, ed., *Archivio capitolare della Cattedrale S. Donato di Pinerolo,* 1984, Word file on the pignerol.altervista.org website, downloaded 20/01/10). He seems to have held these posts until 1623, his probable date of death. In 1599 he was granted the right to absolve heretics. In May 1612 he founded a canonicate in the collegiate church of St. Donatus which his family was to retain until the late 19th century. (Various sources found on the Internet including the Archivio di Stato, Turin.) He must have been a classmate of Piscina.

4 The name of Malabaila, Malabayla or Malabajla, is that of an important family from Asti who were powerful businessmen and money-lenders in the 13th-14th centuries and then rose to nobility, becoming Lords of Canale and other places. Daniele Malabaila (d. 1617?) graduated as a lawyer at Bologna in 1568 (Maria Teresa Guerrini, *"Qui voluerit in iure promoveri...": i dottori in diritto nello Studio di Bologna (1501-1796),* Bologna, 2005, p. 247, no. 2160), became a Count in 1571, and was made Count of Canale in 1604. His son Filippo Malabaila (1580-1657) was a Cistercian Abbott, writer and historian.

5 Francesco Belli was the son of Pietrino (or Pierino, or Perino) Belli (1502-1575), a soldier and jurist from Alba, who served Duke Emanuele Filiberto of Savoy and is credited with publishing the first manual of military law (*De re militari et bello tractatus*, Venice, 1563). Francesco was his first legitimate son, born after his father's marriage in 1541, before his sister Ottavia, and his younger brother Domenico (1548-1601), who was to be Grand Chancellor of Savoy briefly (1600-01), a post to be held later by Francesco Piscina's own son, Giovanni Giacomo. Of Francesco we only know that he worked as a lawyer with his father, and was involved in a boundary settlement dispute between Tuscany and Modena in 1567. In 1568 he was awarded the Papal Order of S. Stefano Papa e Martire (Lodovico Araldi, *L'Italia nobile*, Venice, 1722), and for this was accused of being bribed. He was briefly exiled

from Piedmont (1568-69). In 1575 he was Grand Chancellor of the Order of S. Stefano in Pisa. He returned to Piedmont in 1585 as a Carthusian monk, and was still living by 1589 (F. Rondolino, "Pietrino Bello, sua vita, suoi scritti", *Miscellanea di Storia Italiana,* XXVIII, 1890, pp. 559-61). Like Piscina himself, along with Rinaldo Ressano and Daniele Malabaila, he was a young man from a well-off Piedmontese family. All were probably fond of Tarot.

6 Piscina is here referring to a comedy called *Gl'Ingannati* (The Deceived), performed for the Accademia degli Intronati in Siena in 1531. The Accademia was founded in 1525 as a society dedicated to literature and the arts, and remains active today. In Act III, scene ii, the innkeepers of the inn of the Mirror and of the inn of the Fool, representing Prudence and Foolishness, have a heated argument in which each tries to convince the main characters to lodge at his inn (Ireneo Sanesi, ed., *Commedie del Cinquecento,* Bari, 1912, vol. I, pp. 355-359). Milanese jurist Andrea Alciato (1492-1550) also calls card number 1 an "innkeeper" (*caupo*) in his list of Tarot trumps (*ΠΑΡΕΡΓΩΝ Juris libri VII posteriores,* Lyon, 1554 (1st ed. 1544), bk. VIII ch. xvi, pp. 72-73).

7 Italian: *Re, Regina, Cavagliero* (now *Cavallo*), *Fante,* the four usual courts in the Tarot pack. The gathering of all four courts of the same suit is here called *brezicola,* a term that was otherwise used in other forms of Tarot, like Minchiate (*versicola, verzicola*) where it meant various sets of high or low consecutive trumps, or sets of courts, of major trumps, etc. Piscina's peculiar meaning was still alive in Turin around 1900 as testified by Alberto Viriglio, "Il giuoco ed il dialetto torinese", *Archivio per lo studio delle tradizioni popolari,* XIX (1900), p. 483: "Gruppo di Re, Dama, Cavallo e Fante : *Barsìgôla,* Piccola bazzica." Note that the anonymous *Discorso* (see p. 55) uses too the same word (as *bergigole*). It crept into French as *brizigole* in Abbé de Marolles' *Regles du iev des tarots* (Nevers, 1637; see Depaulis 2002). The role Piscina assigns to the Fool, played as a wild card to complete a set of courts, was hitherto unnoticed, and has not survived in modern forms of Piedmontese Tarot (18th-19th centuries). As Franco Pratesi and Giordano Berti have observed, this rule can however be compared to a similar practice in the Tarocchino Bolognese, where not only the Fool but also the Bagat may substitute for missing cards in combinations. It seems this same rule was observed in France too, since it can be found in the earliest German rules, which faithfully followed French usage. Thus, in the *Regeln bey dem Taroc-Spiele* (Leipzig, 1754), we read: "8. Dieser Excuse wird bey 3 Königen zum 4ten, und bey 3 Bildern zur halben Cavallerie gemachet." (This Fool will make a fourth together with three Kings, or with three court cards, a 'half-cavalry'.) This rule would thus belong to common stock, and would not be specifically Bolognese.

8 Although not clearly stated, this seems to allude to a rule in the game where the four Papal and Imperial cards – i.e. trumps 2 to 5 – are treated as being of equal rank. For Dummett and McLeod (Dummett/McLeod 2004) it is "an exclusively Bolognese characteristic". In Bologna, if more than one such trump is played to a trick and no

higher trump is played, that played last beats the others. The same rule was followed in Piedmont and Savoy, and it is still so in Asti.

9 Boniface VIII (Benedetto Caetani, r. 1294-1303), who wanted to put forward his claims to power "over kings and kingdoms," entered into conflict with the Habsburg Emperor Albert I and, especially, with King Philip IV "the Fair" of France (r. 1285-1314), who, after much quarrelling, sent an army to Anagni, the Pope's residence, which captured and beat him severely (the "Outrage of Anagni", 1303). Clement VII (Giulio di Giuliano de' Medici, r. 1523-1534) had to face the terrible attack and pillage of Rome that Emperor Charles V's army, led by Charles of Bourbon, committed in May 1527 (the "Sack of Rome"). The memory of this attack – a great shock to Western civilisation – was still vivid in 1565.

10 Aristotle provides his definition of justice in *Nicomachean Ethics*, Book V.

11 A reference to Pausanias' speech in Plato's *Symposium*. Answering Phaedrus, Pausanias says: "The Love which is the offspring of the common Aphrodite is essentially common, and has no discrimination, being such as the meaner sort of men feel, and is apt to be of women as well as of youths, and is of the body rather than of the soul – the most foolish beings are the objects of this love which desires only to gain an end, but never thinks of accomplishing the end nobly, and therefore does good and evil quite indiscriminately" (trans. Benjamin Jowett).

12 Ludovico Ariosto, *Orlando Furioso,* Canto III, stanza 37.

13 Cintio Giambattista Giraldi (1504-1573); was born in Ferrara, where he studied medicine and philosophy. In 1541 he was appointed to the chair of rhetoric, and shortly after Duke Ercole II D'Este named him as his secretary. In the following years he composed the nine tragedies that are considered to be his main work. In 1563, he was called by Duke Emanuele Filiberto of Savoy to teach rhetoric in the recently founded University of Mondovì. In 1566, he followed the University to Turin but soon left and, from 1568 to 1571, he taught rhetoric in Pavia. He then returned to Ferrara, where he died in 1573 (Giannandrea Barotti, *Memorie istoriche di letterati ferraresi,* vol. 1, Ferrara, 1792; Pierre-Louis Ginguené, *Storia della letteratura italiana,* vol. 8, Milan, 1824). Giraldi and the Intronati (see note 6) are also mentioned by Alberto Lollio in his *Invettiva… contra il giuoco del tarocco*, and in Vincenzo Imperiali's *Risposta* (c.1550), as transcribed by Girolamo Zorli on his Tretre website (Zorli 2010).

14 Sappho quoted by Aristotle in *Rhetoric*, Book II: "Death is an evil; the gods have judged it to be so; otherwise they would not have preferred immortality" (trans. John Gillies).

15 Francesco Petrarca, *I Trionfi,* Trionfo della Fama, "quando, mirando intorno su per l'erba, / vidi da l'altra parte giunger quella / che trae l'uom del sepolcro e 'n vita il serba." ("when, gazing around through the meadow, / I saw coming from the other side her / who takes the man out of the grave, and preserves him alive").

16 Plato, *The Apology of Socrates:* "Socrates: Now what are spirits or demigods? Are they not either gods or the sons of gods? Is that true? — Meletus: Yes, that is true" (trans. Benjamin Jowett).

17 Apparently the design of the World card known to Piscina offered the symbols of the four Evangelists in the corners, as it does in the Tarot de Marseille. Does this mean this overall design was already known in Piedmont in the 16th century, as it was to be after 1700 when the Tarot de Marseille was imitated by Savoyard and Piedmontese cardmakers? (For this, see Depaulis 2005.) It is hard to say, when we read that "the Fool in the game of Tarot [is] represented in such a way that he looks behind towards a mirror", a representation that is not found in any Tarot design, and that "the Bagat [is] dressed as an innkeeper", which is nowhere the case.

18 Chapters 20-24 of Marsilio Ficino's commentary on Plato's *Timaeus* discuss the properties of the number four from the mathematical, philosophical, physical and metaphysical point of view. (Marsilio Ficino, *Opera Omnia*, Basel, 1576, facsimile reprint, Turin, 1959.)

19 Piscina's *tarocchamente* is an adverb of his own coinage that is based on a meaning of *tarocco* that has the sense of "idiot" or "imbecile". It is the same understanding of the word *tarocco* that Francesco Berni expressed in his *Capitolo del gioco della Primiera* (1526): "...che altro non vuol dir Tarocco che ignocco, sciocco, Balocco..." ("... that the only signification of this word Tarocco is stupid, foolish, simple...", trans. Kaplan 1978, p. 28). The earliest attestation of this sense of the word seems to be the macaronic poet Bassano Mantovano (d. 1499), who used *tarochus* to mean "idiot" or "imbecile" in his poem known simply as *Maccheronea del Bassano* (ll. 34-36, various editions; the edition of Carlo Cordié, "I maccheronici prefolenghiani," in *Opere di Teofilo Folengo,* vol. I, Milan, 1977, pp. 999-1000, spells it *tarocus*).

Discorso perche fusse trouato il
giuoco, et particolarmente quello
del Tarocco: doue si dichiara à pieno il significato
di tutte le figure
di esso giuoco.

Il giuoco fu ritrouato per passatempo, et diporto degli huomini otiosi, et per ricreatione in particolare de sig.ri et altri ancora, che abbondino di facoltà, et ricchezze non mediocri, dopo hauer fatto però
le facende, che à ciascuno secondo l'esser suo, si conuengono, che si bene in
quei primi tempi, come ci mostra il nome, non fu uitio, si è poi nondimeno
à poco à poco dilatato, et della uolontà
degli huomini di modo impadronito

Discorso perchè fosse trovato il giuoco et particolarmente quello del Tarocco…
Paris, Bibliothèque de l'Arsenal, Mss. 8574, p. 1641

Introduction to the Anonymous *Discorso*

With this second *Discorso* we have to face a number of problems, most of them unsolved. The text is known only in manuscript, it is unsigned, and undated. It is here printed, translated and annotated for the first time. The only positive point is that the author follows the "B" order of the Tarot trumps, and can thus be assigned to the Ferrara (or 'Eastern') tradition. We will however see that he is probably not Ferrarese.

In terms of content, the *Discorso perche fosse trovato il giuoco et particolarmente quello del Tarocco* presents several contrasts to Piscina's. It is much more formal and impersonal, with no dedication and very little use of the first person. Unlike Piscina, who composed his work, as he said, on a "whim", the anonymous author deliberately composed his work to fill a gap in the moralizing literature on games. He begins with a historical context, placing the origin of three families of games in ancient times, and offers a Greek etymology for the word *tarocco*. He uses many more historical and literary examples than Piscina to illustrate his interpretation, and spends much more time discussing the meaning of the suits, which he explains as being related to the four "goals of human life" – riches, arms, literature, and pleasure.

The anonymous author describes the subject-matter of the trumps as the "affects and passions that triumph over men." He divides them into two classic ethical divisions: the "active life", from the Fool to the Devil, subordinated to the "contemplative life", from the Heavens to the World, or macrocosm. Within these two divisions, the Anonymous, like Piscina, explains how the trumps succeed one another by logical and moral necessity, "in order to make everyone know his passions and his errors and, leaving aside vanity and the very short and harmful pleasures, to raise his mind to the contemplation of God."

It is again to Franco Pratesi that we owe the discovery of the *Discorso perche fosse trovato il giuoco et particolarmente quello del Tarocco*. It was in fact his first great find to be published in *The Playing-Card* (Pratesi 1987a in the Bibliography). In his article Pratesi presented two manuscripts, one in the Biblioteca Nazionale Centrale, in Florence, another in the Bologna University Library. Around the same time one of us (TD) had just found a third copy in Paris, in the Bibliothèque de l'Arsenal. The 'discoverers' had

both enthusiastically written to Michael Dummett to inform him of their respective finds. Franco Pratesi's article had already been sent to the IPCS journal, and it was too late to include the Paris materials, which have so far remained undisclosed.[1]

A few years later Lucia Nadin mentioned a fourth copy held in the Vatican Library at Rome in her book *Carte da gioco e letteratura tra Quattrocento e Ottocento*,[2] and we have recently found a fifth copy in the catalogues of the Österreichische Nationalbibliothek in Vienna.

We now know of five copies of the same text, all hand-written (by different hands). None seems to be autograph. We list them here.

- 'Del Giuoco del Tarocco', Florence, Biblioteca Nazionale Centrale, ms. G. Capponi 24, ff. 344-362:[3]
  This manuscript used to belong to Gino Capponi (Florence 1792-1876), who bequeathed his books and manuscripts to the library in 1876. A quick survey of the other texts grouped under the same heading "Codice XXIV" shows that they are political discourses dealing with matters dated between c.1540 and c.1585. The Tarot text comes at the end of the volume.

- 'Discorso perchè fosse trovato il giuoco et particolarmente quello del Tarocco...', Paris, Bibliothèque de l'Arsenal, Mss. 8574, pp. 1641-83:[4]
  Vols. 8573 and 8574 are twin volumes containing mainly Venetian dispatches and diplomatic reports dating between 1526 and 1579, though a majority are dated between 1554 and 1579. All were copied by the same elegant, professional hand probably in the early 17th century. The volumes were formerly in the collection of Valentin Conrart (1603-1675), the first 'perpetual secretary' of the Académie française.

- 'Discorso perchè fosse trovato il gioco et particolarmente quello del Tarocco...', Vienna, Österreichische Nationalbibliothek, ms. 6750, 37, ff. 398a-411b:[5]
  The Austrian Library catalogue describes this copy as: "Discorso perchè fosse troua-

---

1 This is the text we publish here.
2 Nadin 1997, pp. 57 and 197.
3 Our *Discorso* is referred to in Carlo Milanesi, *Catalogo dei manoscritti posseduti dal Marchese Gino Capponi*, Florence, 1845, p. 244 (Cose varie), as "2065. Discorso sul giuoco dei Tarocchi. CODICE XXIV, car. 344-362." See also Pratesi 1987a.
4 See A. Marsand, *I manoscritti italiani delle regie biblioteche di Parigi*, Paris, 1838, II, p. 325 (no. 57 - 954); G. Mazzatinti, *Inventario dei manoscritti italiani delle biblioteche di Francia*, Paris, 1888, III, p. 145 ("n° 57 - 8573-8574, sec. XVII; Relazioni delle corti europee (1544-1576) d'ambasciatori veneti").
5 Academia Caesarea Vindobonensis, *Tabulae codicum manu scriptorum praeter graecos et orientales in Bibliotheca Palatina Vindobonensi asservatorum*, V, Vienna, 1871, p. 64, No. 6750, 37.

to il gioco et particolarmente quello del Tarocco doue se dichiara a pieno il significato de tutte le figure di esso giocco. / Incip.: 'Il Cioco [sic] fu ritrouato per passatempo'. / Expl.: 'di tutto quello che nell'huomo, il quale è un picciol mondo, si
contiene'." Vol. no. 6750 [Fosc. 179] is a thick compendium containing documents
in Italian from various sources, with dates spanning between 1543 and 1625.

- 'Discorso perchè fosse trouato il Giuoco et particolarmente quello del
  Tarocco...', Bologna, Biblioteca Universitaria, ms. 1072, vol. XIII.F:[6]
  A poor, hastily written copy. Filippo-Maria Monti (Bologna 1675-Rome 1754),
  in whose collection this manuscript used to be, was made cardinal in 1743. He
  donated his valuable library to the University of Bologna. Ms. 739 (1072) is a
  large collection of XV volumes comprising pieces of all sorts in Italian from various sources; dated documents show 1536, 1574, 1589, 1655.

- 'Del Giuoco del Tarocco', Rome, Biblioteca Apostolica Vaticana, ms.
  Urb. lat. 856, pt. I, n° 12, f. 168-176, dated 1657.[7]

It was Franco Pratesi's opinion that "the date of the original draft is the
second half of the sixteenth century",[8] a dating we not only agree with but
can refine to the mid-1560's for reasons to be explained below. As for the
place of origin, Pratesi was much more hesitant, – as we still are! – balanc-
ing between Venice and Rome, two cities we nonetheless prefer to rule out.
Pratesi tried to draw a conclusion from the currencies that are mentioned in
the text, which he read as "ducati" and "soldi" (for, actually, *scudi*). But
almost all Italian states have in fact minted *ducati* as well as *scudi*, and it is
impossible to infer anything from these denominations. The dispersal of the
five manuscripts – Florence, Rome, Bologna, but also Paris and Vienna, with
no clear initial provenance – is a second dead end. It would have been easier
to localize if the copies were in collections with a more regional scope.

Our dating relies mainly on the identification of some of the books the
anonymous author mentions, quotes or alludes to. One which is quoted
extensively is Pliny's *Natural history*, as translated by Cristoforo Landino, a
version that was first printed in Venice in 1476 and many times reissued,

---

6 See *Inventari dei manoscritti delle biblioteche d'Italia,* vol. XIX (1912), p. 116:
"Bologna, R. Biblioteca universitaria, 739 (1072), vol. XIII, F. Discorso perchè fosse
trovato il giuoco, et particolarmente quello del Tarocco, dove si dichiara a pieno il
significato di tutte le figure di esso giuoco. (...) (ms. cart., fol., sec. XVII, prov. dal
card. Filippo Monti)."; also Pratesi 1987a; Berti/Vitali 1987, no. 46 (with date "ca.
1570").

7 The only dated copy! This manuscript is mentioned (and quoted for a few lines)
in Nadin 1997, p. 57 fn. 28 and p. 197 fn. 53. See also Cosmo Stormajolo, *Codices
urbinates latini,* II, Rome, 1912, p. 523.

8 Pratesi 1987a, p. 81.

until 1543. Yet, in 1561, Lodovico Domenichi had published a new, very different and much more modern translation, which was immediately reprinted the following year, and again in 1573, 1580, 1589, until the early 17th century.[9] It is clear that our anonymous author always uses Landino's translation, not Domenichi's. This is why we believe the text cannot have been written much after 1565/70.

Can we determine a *terminus a quo*? We have seen that the anonymous author prefers quoting ancient writers in Italian rather than in Latin. (Indeed, in spite of so many references to Latin literature, there is not a Latin word in this text, and we may even suppose its author did not know Latin.) Galen is mentioned at the very beginning of the text, as *Galeno*, suggesting it is the Italian translation which is here referred to, not the Latin one. Although Galen's treatise on the ball game was first translated from Greek into Latin in 1533, its first Italian translation did not appear, in Milan, before 1562.[10] It is our assumption that it is this 1562 edition which is alluded to, and therefore that the *Discorso* was written after this date, and, as we have seen, not much later. The other identified sources are earlier.[11]

The problem of the provenance is much more complex. It has been pointed out, first by Pratesi, that the *Discorso* lists the Tarot trumps in the "B" (Ferrarese or 'Eastern') order, but departs from its 'canon' by some irregularities which lead us to think the author was living neither in Ferrara nor in Venice. Comparing lists as drawn from various sources (the late-15th century Steele Sermon, Aretino's *Pasquinata ... per il conclave e l'elezione di Adriano VI* of 1522, Troilo Pomeran's *Triomphi ... composti sopra li terocchi in laude delle famose gentil donne di Vinegia* of 1534, Alessandro Citolini's *La Tipocosmia*, 1561, and others) shows that the anonymous *Discorso* interchanges the places of the Chariot and Fortitude, a rather unusual situation, and has Prudence instead of Temperance. Among the Papi neither the Popess nor the Empress is present!

Since our lists come from Ferrara and from Venice, where the B order seems to have been followed without much change, we are tempted to conclude that our anonymous author was from elsewhere. (Had he been Venetian, he would furthermore have spelt the game as *terocchi*, as all

---

9 *Historia naturale di G. Plinio Secondo, tradotta per M. Lodouico Domenichi con le postule in margine*, Venice, 1561; reprinted 1562, 1573, 1580, 1589, 1603, 1612.

10 *Il libro di Claudio Galeno Dell'esercizio della palla nuovamente tradotto della lingua Latina nella nostra volgare*, Milan, 1562.

11 See our detailed comments.

Venetian sources do.) This leaves us with a few other areas, like Trento – but neither the order of the trumps nor the language are comparable to that used in Trento[12] –, Mantua and Modena. Modena being ruled by the Estes, it is reasonable to suppose that Tarot was played there the same way as in Ferrara, and there are good reasons to think Mantua followed similar practices. As for Rome it is assumed that a local writer would have used an "A" (or 'Southern') type of order, as all Roman witnesses confirm.

Can we infer anything from the language? In the 16th century Italy was still looking for a standard literary language whose model was being built up by the Florentines. Although Tuscan authors were setting the tone, not all Italian writers wanted or were able to write the same way. Even those who were close to the Florentine model kept a few regional idioms, or had their own local spelling. It is in search of such clues that we received the help of Mme Claire Lesage, assistant professor of Italian at the University of Rennes (France), whom we wholeheartedly thank. She confirms what had struck some of us (and Girolamo Zorli as well): it is a good, learned, 'near-standard' Italian, with almost no regional flavour. Claire Lesage calls it a "Tuscanized" language (but definitely not "Tuscan").

More surprisingly, while she pointed out a few typical terms or spellings that clearly belong to a "northern" tradition (like *fassi* for *fasci*, p. 1654, or single consonants where double should be used), there are some "southern" forms, like *ghianne* for *ghiande*, *mazze* for *bastoni*, or *de* for *di*, and many doubled consonants, a phenomenon, she tells us, which is common in the South of Italy, not in the North. All in all this is a text that mixes traits from northern and southern usages. Even if we have to be cautious because none of the manuscripts we have seen is the original version, and copyists may have introduced their own spellings, we are inclined to think the author was indeed from these central regions that include the Marches, Umbria, and Lazio, where influences from the North (which starts in Emilia-Romagna) and from the South (Abruzzo, Molise) are mingled. Having southern forms mixed with northern borrowings is a feature of these central dialects, such as Marchigiano or Romanesco.[13]

If we rule out Rome for the above-mentioned reasons, we may look

---

12 As exemplified by Leonardo Colombino's *Il Trionfo tridentino* (1547). See Patrizia Cordin, "Il Trionfo tridentino di Leonardo Colombino", in *Cultura d'élite e cultura popolare nell'arco alpino fra Cinque e Seicento,* Ottavio Besomi and Carlo Caruso, ed., Basel, 1995, pp. 173-189.

13 For this discussion, see Devoto/Giacomelli 1972 (Marche), Bruni 1992 and 1994.

towards the Marches: it is a coastal region, not far from Ferrara, and the so-called "northern Marchigiano" dialect – spoken in Pesaro and Urbino – belongs to the same Emilian-Romagnolo group as Ferrarese. Although *mazze* is the most common word for the Baton suit in southern Italy, and is still used in Naples and Sicily, in lieu of the standard *bastoni*, we were fortunate to discover that it was also used in Pesaro in the 16th century.[14]

It may be surprising to find Pesaro here, but Pesaro had some special link with the Tarot, at least during Alessandro Sforza's reign over the city (1445-1473). One of the rare sets of illuminated Tarot cards, now preserved in Catania (Sicily), offers on its king of Swords what appears to be the emblem of Alessandro Sforza, Lord of Pesaro.[15]

However, this is only one hypothesis among others, less credible. Much remains to be done to identify the place where the Anonymous *Discorso* was written and, if we ever succeed in this, to identify its hidden author.

Although we are confident, as the foregoing discussion has made clear, that the date of the Anonymous *Discorso* must be only shortly after 1562, the other two questions, provenance and authorship, remain to be settled with any degree of certainty. We hope that the tentative steps we have made in their direction will inspire further research on this fascinating document.

Addendum 2018

A sixth copy of the Anonymous Discourse was discovered in 2011 by one of us in a manuscript collection, dated 1584, offered for sale by the Parisian bookseller Emile Dufossé, in a catalogue titled *Americana: catalogue de livres relatifs à l'Amérique, Europe, Asie, Afrique et Océanie*. Paris, Librairie ancienne et moderne E. Dufossé, n.d. (c.1880):

> • "26787. MANUSCRIT autographe signé de Giulio Pallavicino (1564-1635), in-4 vélin de 600 pp., 1584 (B.) 60 fr. Mélange très intéressant, contient les relations suivantes: (...) 4. Discorso perché fosse trovato il giuoco et particolarmente quello del Tarocco, dove si dichiara a pieno il significato di tutte le figure di esso giuoco. – (...)." (p. 398).

Whether the book was sold, and to whom, is currently lost to history. Upon our inquiry, the major Pallavicino collection at the Archivio Storico del Comune di Genova searched their manuscripts and kindly informed us that they had found nothing corresponding to this description.

---

14 In a short nonsensical poem made of playing-card terms ("una specie di indovinello, in istile mezzo burchiellesco") which is part of a musical manuscript made up near Pesaro during the 16th century, and now kept in the Pesaro City Library (Alfredo Saviotti, "Di un codice musicale del secolo XVI", *Giornale storico della letteratura italiana*, XIV, 1889, pp. 234-53, here pp. 235-6).

15 This identification was made by Giuliana Algeri in Berti/Vitali 1987, no. 2, pp. 32-33. It was however much disputed by Enrica Domenicali who explains the cards were made for Borso d'Este. But it is certain that Borso did "license" his emblem to Sforza.

Our edition

We give here the text of the manuscript which is in the Bibliothèque de l'Arsenal, Paris. It is a good copy, with few errors, and very legible writing. It is much better in any case than the Bologna copy and is comparable to the Florence copy. Because we do not intend to publish a "critical edition" of the text – which would require comparing all five manuscripts and scrupulously giving all text variants, including minor ones –, we have limited ourselves to a selection of the most significant differences. The spelling of the Bologna copy (B) is closer to modern Italian spelling standards than the Florence (F) and Paris (A) copies. For example, when A reads *"avaritia di vil mercantia"*, B has *"avarizia di vil mercanzia"*. A's *"inclinatione"* is B's *"inclinazione"*, etc. Often we find a c in A, while F has a *t*, and B has a *z*, e.g. A *giudicio* / F *giuditio* / B *giudizio*, or A *precioso* / F *pretioso* / B *pretioso*. A writes *contemplation* while F has *contemplatione* and B, *contemplazione*. The Arsenal copy has a tendency toward Latinized erudite spelling, like *havevano* (B *avevano*), Horatio (B Orazio), Hortensio (B Ortensio), Monarcha (B Monarca), but has Petrarca (B Petrarcha).

To provide an easier reading, abbreviations have been developed, e.g. *mag^r* is rendered as *mag[gio]r*, *Imp^{re}* as *Imp[erato]re*, *qa^{li}* as *q[u]ali*, etc.

Comments refer to the English translation, and are placed after it, as we have done for Piscina's *Discorso*.

[p. 1641]
Discorso perche fosse trovato il
giuoco et particolarmente quello
del Tarocco : dove si dichia:
ra a pieno il significato
di tutte le figure
di esso giuoco.

&

Il giuoco fu ritrovato per passatempo et diporto degli huomini otiosi, et
per ricreatione in particolare de Sig[no]ri et altri ancora che abbondino di
facoltà et ricchezze non mediocri, dopo haver fatto però le faccende che a
ciascuno secondo l'esser suo, si convengono ; che si bene in quei primiᵃ tempi
come ci mostra il nome, non fù vitio, si è poi nondimeno a poco a poco
dilatato et della volontà degli huomini di modoᵇ impadronato [p. 1642] che
non più giuoco, né spasso ma dispiacere, vitio, et rovinaᶜ si può dire, poiche
quindi si vedono ogni giorno manifeste perdite non pur di facoltà ma del-
l'istessa riputatione, et bene spesso dell'anima et del corpo insieme. Perche
non più per trattenimento, ma per avaritia di vil mercantia si essercita et così
dispiacevole si è ridotto a brutto et dishonesto fine. Et nondimeno in tale
abuso salito vedi che fa la mala consuetudine, et inclinatione degli huomini
che per vile et da poco si accenna chi non giuoca: la onde più a questo, che
in diverse maniere si frequenta, che a qualsivoglia arte ò scienza con ogni studio et diligenza si attende, et colui che / [p. 1643] assai giuoca, et nome di
bello et gran giocatore, si acquista, sia pur di che conditione si voglia, che
sopra ogni altro da Principi è favorito et accarezzato.

Tre furono i giuochi dagli antichi principali per spasso et trattenimento
ritrovati, et posti in uso, lo Scacco, la Palla et il Tarocco. Nello Scacco si
mostra l'acutezza dell' ingegno et quasi insegna l'arte militare. Nella Palla la
forza et agilità del corpo. Nel Tarocco la vita attiva et contemplativa. Del
primo scrissero molti et massime il Vida Cremonese in versi heroici. Del secondo oltre agli altri Galeno. Del terzo mi maraviglio certo che piu diffusa-
mente non sia stato / [p. 1644] scritto, essendo questo degli altri piu utile et
piu bello perche sicome per la sua varietà et diverse figure et personaggi che
ci intervengono è molto vago et dilettevole cosi anco per la sua inventione si
rende grato mirabile et utile per gli ammaestramenti della vita humana, tutto
il corso della quale se ci vede et dottamente, et artificiosamente compreso et

---

a B "primi" *added above the line as a correction*
b B del mondo *[sic]*
c F ruina

A Discourse on why game-playing,
and Tarot in particular, was
invented, in which the
meaning of all
the figures of
that game is
completely
explained.

Game-playing was invented as a pastime and amusement for idle people, and in particular for the diversion of Lords and others who have plenty
of means and riches beyond the average, after they have accomplished
those duties that are assigned to everyone according to their status. Though
at the beginning it was not a vice, as proved by the name, later it gradually
spread out and began to influence the will of the people in such a way, that
now it cannot be considered a game or a diversion anymore, but a dis-
pleasure, a vice, and a ruin; because every day we clearly see the loss not
only of money, but of reputation itself, and frequently of the soul and body
together. The game is no longer played for entertainment, but for the greed
of vile merchandise, and is now unhappily reduced to an ugly and dishonest purpose.

You can observe how it is arisen to such an abuse, causing evil habits and
inclinations in men, who consider those who do not play to be vile and
worthless. So this is frequented more, and with greater attention and diligence, than any art or science; and whoever plays much, and obtains the
fame of being a beautiful and great player, whatever his condition may be, is
favoured and cherished by Princes more than anyone else.

There were three main games that the ancients invented and put in use
for their diversion and entertainment: Chess, Ball, and Tarot. In Chess clever-
ness and ingenuity are displayed, and it almost teaches military art. In Ball,
the strength and agility of the body. In Tarot, the active and the contemplative life.[1] Many have written about the first one, most of all Vida of Cremona,
in heroic verses.[2] About the second one, Galen,[3] among others. I wonder why
more has not been written[4] about the third one, this being the noblest of
them all and also the most beautiful: it is very pleasant and delightful for the
variety of its different figures and characters, but it is also appreciable for its
conception, wonderful and useful in the teachings of human life, whose
whole course is wisely and cleverly represented and explained. Because all

esplicato. Et sicome l'attioni humane tutte sono indrizzate ad uno[a] di questi quattro fini, cioè all' acquisto delle ricchezze ò all' armi, ò alle lettere, overo alli piaceri ; cosi fù il giuoco dal prudentissimo Authore principalmente in quattro parti diviso, cioè in Danari, Spade,[b] Mazze, / [p. 1645] et Coppe, et instituito il giuoco in quattro, se ben hora per lo più si giuoca in terzo, sendo il numero quaternario degli altri più perfetto, poiche havendo in se il tre, il due et l'uno viene a comprendere il dieci ; il qual numero contiene et numera tutti gli altri numeri, poiche le centinaia, et le migliaia non sono altro che quantità de decine et perciò la sagace natura secondo questo num[e]ro ordinò le prime qualità veri principij di tutte le cose naturali dalle quali risultano i quattro Elementi, et da questi i quattro humori del n[ost]ro corpo, et quindi le temperature, secondo le quali derivano i costumi et inclinationi dai quattro sopradetti / [p. 1646] fini:[c] dalla variatione di quattro humori sortiscono anco le quattro età della vita nostra, alle quali corrispondono i quattro tempi dell'anno, et in quattro tempi sono anco de i corpi humani l'infirmità distinte. Ma per dichiarare a parte a parte et per ordine i vaghi et acuti misterij che sotto queste carte si contengono cominceró dal nome.

Tarocco in lingua Greca altro non vuol dire, che salso, et precioso condimento, nome veramente conveniente et proprio sendo questo di diverse cose fatto un concime saporito d'acutezze et giovevoli contemplationi ripieno et perciò precioso et solo tra tutti gli altri degno d'esser tenuto in pregio / [p. 1647] sendo tutti gli altri a paragone di questo sciocchi et d'inventione privi et di giudicio, che ad altro non tendono, che a fine pernicioso, et brutto.

Fù il Tarocco il primo giuoco che di Carte si trovasse, sotto quattro Re instituito secondo che a quattro fini universali si indrizzano le volontà[d] et attioni humane, i quali poi si conchiudono in un solo del piacere, nel quale fu dagli Epicuri posto il sommo bene et in ciascuno di quattro distinse l'Authore, Re, Regina, Cavalieri, et Fanti, nelle persone ~~proprie~~ de q[u]ali dinota tutte le dignità dell'uno et l'altro sesso, dalla Reale sino al privato gentilhuomo, et dal dieci sino all'uno,[e] con il qual numero si com: / [p. 1648] putano gli altri numeri, ponendo il finito per l'infinito volle significare tutti gli altri huomini descendendo sempre da quelli di maggiore auttorità agli inferiori, sin' a coloro che sendo al Mondo solo per far numero sono detti Assi.

Il primo Re dunque, dietro al quale con sete insatiabile d'havere corre la mag[gio]r parte, è quello de Danari senza i quali parendo, che al mondo non

a B le attioni humane tutte ad uno (*missing* "sono indrizzate")
b Spade *added above the line*
c B et inclinazioni. Dalli quali quattro sopradetti fini
d F s' indrizzano le volontà / B s'indirizzano le volontà
e B dell'uno, con il qual numero (missing "et l'altro sesso... sino all'uno")

human actions are directed to one of these four goals – the gaining of riches, the use of arms, literature, or pleasure – so the very prudent author divided the game into four main parts, that is coins, swords, maces[5] and cups; and the game was instituted for four,[6] even if it is now mainly played by three, because the quaternary number is more perfect than the others, since, having in itself three, two and one, it comes to include ten. Ten contains and numbers all other numbers, since hundreds and thousands are but quantities of tens. So wise nature ordered according to this number the first qualities in the principles of all natural things from which the four Elements result, and from these, the four humours of our body, and then the temperaments, according to which customs and inclinations derive from the above-mentioned four goals. From the variations in the four humours, the four ages of our life are produced: to them, the four times of the year correspond. Also, illnesses in human bodies are divided into four times. But, in order to explain in a detailed and orderly way the beautiful and acute mysteries that are contained in these cards, I will begin with the name.

In the Greek language, "Tarocco" means a salty and precious sauce.[7] It is a truly fitting and appropriate name, since it is made of different things, as a tasty condiment, full of incisive and healthy contemplations: this is why it is so precious and the only one among the others that is worthy to be held in grace, since, when compared with this one, all the others are foolish and lacking in invention or wisdom, and aimed only towards a bad and pernicious goal.

Tarot was the first card game to be invented,[8] established under four Kings, because human action and will tend to four universal ends, which are all included in pleasure, which the Epicureans[9] consider as the highest good. In each of them, the author distinguished King, Queen, Knights and Pages, in which persons he denotes all the dignity of the one and the other sex, from the Royal to the private gentleman, and from ten to one, the number from which all the others are calculated. Placing the finite for the infinite, he wanted to signify all the other men, always descending from those of higher authority to the inferior, down to those that, being in the world only to be counted, are called Aces.

So the first King, behind whom most of the people run with inextinguishable greed, is that of Coins: without them, it seems that nobody in the world can be said to be happy. From the highest dignity down to the lowest commoner, every one of them tries as much as he can to accumulate money, and to have it in abundance, saying that honours, commodity and the capacity to

si possa dire huomo beato, dalla suprema dignità sino alla bassa plebe, ciascuno di questi si sforza più che può di accumularli[a] et haverne copia, dicendo, che da questi dipendono gli honori le commodità et il poter trarsi ogni
sua voglia, anzi che parer fanno / [p. 1649] prudentiss[im]i et savij i pazzi,
belli i brutti, dotti gli ignoranti,[b] et colmi di virtù i vitiosi. Et per il contrario
li virtuosi dotti, et savij senza quattrini di pochissima riputatione et stima al
che havendo risguardo il Petrarca disse:
"Povera et nuda vai filosofia."
Et di lui prima Horatio:
"Cercate i danar prima o Cittadini
Et dopò questi le virtù cercate."
La sete di quest'oro aguzza l'ingegno humano a solcare il Mare et commettersi[c] in poco legno all'instabilità de' venti et dell'onde per accumularlo.
Ad altri è stato causa di rompere la data fede per haverlo.
Ad altri di commettere homicidij nel proprio sangue. / [p. 1650] Ad alcu-
ni di far venale il proprio honore. Ad alcuni altri[d] non haver rispetto ancora
alli sacri Tempij. Polinestore Re di Thracia ammazzò Polidoro giovanetto
sotto la data fede a Priamo di servarlo per haver l'oro che haveva portato
seco. Pigmalione, Re di Tiri[e] ammazzò il cognato Sicheo per possedere il suo
Tesoro. Catone Uticense tanto severo, et savio concesse la propria moglie ad
Hortensio perchè la lasciasse de suoi bene herede. Marco Crasso la terza
volta che fù console rapì due mila libre di oro dall' Altare di Giove
Capitolino, ne di questo anco satiò, ne di tanto et tanto altro, che ne possede-
va nella guerra contro i Parthi dove egli fù Imperatore, / [p. 1651] cupido più
di riportar ricchezze, che d'acquistar gloria, fù ammazzato et tagliatagli la
testa fù posta in un vaso d'oro colato così dicendo:
"Dell'oro havesti sete, hor bevi l'oro".
Di maniera che con Virgilio si può dire:
"Et che nó può dell'oro la sacra fame".[f]
Hor non potendo l'ingordo appetito in quei primi tempi satiarsi d'accumular danari, et ricchezze a suo volere, oltre à mille inganni, et modi incon-
venienti ritrovò l'uso dell'armi et della guerra, con le quali coloro, che di più
cuore, et maggior forza, furono, degli altrui beni violentemente si
impadronirono, et quindi a poco a poco nacquero le Signorie et le divisioni

a F d'accomularli / B d'accumularne
b B *(inverted order)* savij i pazzi, e colmi di virtù li viziosi, belli i brutti, e dotti
gl'Ignoranti
c B a solcare, e commettersi *(missing* "il Mare")
d B Ad altri *(missing* "Ad alcuni di far venale il proprio honore".) F Ad alcun' altri
e *Sic for* Tiro
f B E che non può dell'or la sacra fame

satisfy any desire depend on it. They make it so that fools seem to be very prudent and wise, the ugly beautiful, the ignorant learned, the vicious full of virtue. And, on the other hand the virtuous, learned and wise that have no money are held in the lowest reputation and esteem. About this, Petrarch wrote:[10]

Philosophy, you go around poor and naked.

And, before him, Horace:[11]

Citizens, you look firstly for money,
and only afterwards for virtue.

The thirst for gold instigates human ingenuity to sail the sea, trusting in little boats, to the instability of winds and waves, in order to gather it. For some, gaining it has been the cause for breaking the given faith.

For others, to commit homicides against their own blood. For some, to make their honour venal. For others, not to respect the sacred temples themselves. Polymestor, King of Thrace, killed young Polydorus,[12] having promised Priam that he would save him in order to have the money he brought with him. Pygmalion,[13] King of Tyre, killed his brother-in-law Sychaeus to acquire his treasure. Cato of Utica,[14] who was so wise and severe, conceded his wife to Hortensius so that she was made heiress of his possessions. The third time that he was consul, Marcus Crassus stole two thousand pounds of gold from the altar of the Capitoline Jupiter:[15] and he was not satisfied by this nor by the many other things he owned. During the war against the Parthians, in which he was *Imperator*, he desired more to gain riches than to acquire glory. He was killed, and his head was cut and put in a vase full of liquid gold, with the pronouncement:

You were thirsty for gold, now drink gold.[16]

So we can say with Virgil:[17]

What is not possible for the cursed hunger for gold.

Since in those early times people could not satiate their appetite for the accumulation of money and riches at their will, a thousand new deceptions and roundabout ways were created, as well as the use of arms and war. Using them, those that had more courage and greater strength seized with violence the goods that belonged to others. As a consequence, Lordships and the division of the world into Empires and Kingdoms gradually began to be born. For the acquisition of them, countless millions of people were killed, with many robberies, fires and destruction of places, without any respect for

del Mondo in Imperij et Regni / [p. 1652] per l'acquisto de quali sono stati ammazzati infiniti milioni d'huomini con tante rapine et tanti incendij et desolationi de luoghi senza alcun risguardo di grado, sangue, ò sesso. Et perciò ne sarà sempre com'anco è stato, sottosopra il Mondo. Et questo sfrenato (?) desiderio è creciuto tanto che si sono trovati figliuoli, che hanno i Padri uccisi per regnare et de Padri si crudeli, che per questo fine hanno sparso il sangue de fig[liuo]li.

Al che havendo l'Authore risguardo pose nel suo gioco nella seconda sede con la sua squadra di Re di spade. Et se bene il mestier dell'armi par che per acquisto d'honore si esserciti, ha nondimeno se meglio / [p. 1653] si considera per proprio fine l'utile, et il guadagno.

Ma perche furono molti a quali non piacque il mestier dell'armi, d'animo nondimeno invitto, et d'acuto ingegno, avidi di gloria et di ricchezze, non potendo soffrire, che la forza et l'audacia solamente reggessero il Mondo, ritrovarono le lettere, le scienze et l'inventioni delle cose con le loro cause et si acquistarono con l'eloquenza nome di savij. Laonde instituirono le Republiche, le dierono le leggi et sotto nome de Magistrati le ressero, et governaronle, et in segno d'honore et grandezza volendo monstrar, che a loro stava il punire, et castigare si facevano portar le mazze / [p. 1654] avanti; che i Romani poi domandarono fassi, et di qui anco adesso si costuma, che i Rettori di publici studij si fanno portare la mazza avanti, et à Generali degli Esserciti si dà il Bastone et così anco a gli Imperatori, et Re nelle loro creationi.

Il che gentilmente è stato sotto il Re di Bastoni espresso nella terza sede locato. Et se bene il fine delle scienze è il sapere, senza denari poco giova et di assai poca riputatione risulta, perciò anco a questo si attende per acquistar ricchezze, per mezo delle quali lo scientiato diventa glorioso, et senza ò poco, ò nulla è risguardato. Delle ricchezze adunque, et posseder / [p. 1655] Tesori all'acquisto de quali per varie vie si come nascono le delitie, et piaceri, et contentezze humane, nelle quali per esserci più che ad altro inclinato l'huomo, non mancarono filosofi, che in ciò posero il sommo bene, et gli attribuirono Bacco per Iddio per essere stato dopò haver superato l'India, et l'Asia molto dissoluto, et nei piaceri immerso, inventor del vino, et del viver delicato et sontuoso, et perciò si dipinge giovane grasso, et sempre rosso in viso, come che spensierato solamente attendesse a prendersi piacere,[a] le cui feste se bene da molti tutto l'anno, nel Carnevale nondimeno sono da tutti universalmente celebrate, / [p. 1656] furono anco da lui nelli suoi Baccanti ritrovate le maschere acciocche ciascuno a suo capriccio senza vergogna secondo che naturalmente era inclinato oprar potesse, acciocche non mancasse

---

a B a prendersi buon tempo, e piacere (*adds* "buon tempo")

status, family or gender. This is why the World will always be upside-down, as it always has been. And this unbounded desire has grown so much that there have been sons that have killed their fathers in order to reign, and fathers that were so cruel that, for this same goal, have spilled the blood of their sons.

Considering this, the author put in the second place of his game the King of Swords with his squad. Even if it seems that the profession of arms is practised in order to gain glory, on more careful consideration, it has for its goal utility and gain.

But there were many who did not like the profession of arms, and who were nevertheless of undefeated spirit and acute intelligence, greedy for glory and riches, and intolerant of the fact that only strength and courage ruled the world: they invented literature, science and the study of things along with their causes. They gained, thanks to their eloquence, the name of wise. So they instituted the Republics, gave laws to them, and ruled and governed them with the name of magistrates. In order to represent their honour and greatness, the fact that only they could punish and castigate, they had maces brought ahead of them. Later, the Romans called these *fasces*. Even today, the Rectors of public matters have a mace brought ahead of them, and a Baton is given to the Generals of the Armies and to Emperors and Kings in their coronations.

This has been appropriately represented with the King of Batons, in the third place. And even if the goal of science is knowledge, without money this is of little use and gives but a very small reputation. So even this is attended in order to gain riches, by means of which the scholar becomes glorious; without them he is held as little or nothing.

From richness and owning treasures, which are acquired in various ways, delight and pleasure and human happiness are born. Since man is mainly inclined to these things, there have been philosophers that put in them the highest good, and they recognized Bacchus as God, since, after travelling through India and Asia, he was very dissolute, and fond of pleasure. He invented wine and the delightful and sumptuous life; this is why he is represented as young, fat and always red in his face, as if he were only interested in giving himself a pleasant time, without worries. There are many who practise his feasts during the whole year, but they are universally celebrated during carnival. In his Bacchanals, he also invented masks, so that anyone could act according to his caprice, following without shame his natural inclination,

cosa alcuna per sodisfare a pieno [?] alle lascivie humane:[a] Et perche fù primo
a quelle genti rozze, che erano solite nodrirsi di ghianne;[b] come fiere di
mostrare nelle sue mense copiose vivande bene acconcie, et pretiosissimi vini
in cambio d'acqua, perciò nei successori del suo nome i gran conviti furon
detti Bacchetti; se bene hora per trascorso di lingua si chiamino Banchetti,
crebbero poi a' tempo di Nino et in maggior uso li ridusse Sarda / [p. 1657]
napalo che ci dissipò quasi tutto il Regno et in ciò tanto si compiacque, che
ne volse anco mostrar segno nella morte, ordinando sopra il suo sepolcro per
memoria cotal detto:
      "Mangia, bevi et giuoca
      Che non è dopo morte alcun piacere".
      Apitio fù famoso perche fù primo che diede a mangiar lingue di papagal-
lo, et il fegato saporitissimo della triglia, la quale perciò poi ascese a tanta
stima che Asinio Celere nel Principato di Claudio ne comprò una otto millia
nummi, che sono della nostra moneta circa cento cinquanta scudi;
Aristossene Cireneo innaffiava le latuche con acqua melata perche di miglior
gusto dive- / [p. 1658] nissero. Sergio Orata fù il primo che ritrovò i vivai del-
l'ostriche a Baia et Curtio delle murene, il quale nella cena trionfale di Cesare
dittatore glie ne presentò sei millia. Lucullo tagliò un monte presso a Napoli
per fare una peschiera in terra ferma d'acqua salsa con maggiore spesa, che
non gli era costo la villa, dopò la cui morte venderono i Pesci, che vi erano
quaranta millia sestertij d'oro che importano 400/m ducati, oltre che nodri-
va varie sorti d'uccelli, et animali selvaggi, in cui sontuosi banchetti fatti in
Apoline, che così dalla statua d'Apollo chiamava quello appartamento, tra-
passarono gli altri / [p. 1659] sin' a quel tempo fatti. Furono celebrati i conviti di Marc'Antonio, et quello di Cleopatra, nel quale si mangiò la Perla di valore di cento millia sestertij, che importano un milione di ducati. Questa
Regina superba, come bella sendo ogni giorno da Marcantonio convitata,
ogni suo apparato per eccellente, che fosse biasimava, perche dimandata da
lui, che più si potesse a suoi conviti aggiungere, rispose ella, che in una cena
consumerebbe cento mila sestertij, giudicò Antonio esserli impossibile, di che
mosse i pegni. Cleopatra il di determinato pose in ordine la cena sontuosa et
Regale, ma non però maggiore di quelle, che a lei ogni / [p. 1660] giorno
apparecchiava Antonio,[c] per il che ridendo gli disse che per gratia gli
mostrasse in che avesse si grossa somma speso; soggiunse lei di nuovo che
prima che la cena finisse, solo si mangierebbe quanto detto haveva: onde

a B per sodisfare alle lascivie humane (*missing* "a pieno")
b B erano state solite et erano [?] nodirsi di ghianda
c B Marc'Antonio apparecchiava

and nothing was missing for the satisfaction of human lasciviousness. He was the first one to show to the rustic peoples, who used to feed on acorns, how to present on their tables abundant and well prepared food, and very precious wines instead of water. Therefore the successors of his name called great feasts "bacchetts", even if now, from changes in the language, they are called "banquets". They grew at the time of Ninus, and were put to the greatest use by Sardanapalus, who almost dissipated his whole kingdom on account of them. He took such pleasure in them that he wanted to show a sign of this also after his death, ordering this sentence as a memorial on his grave:[18]

Eat, drink and play,

For after death there is no pleasure.

Apicius was famous because he was the first one to offer as food parrot tongues and the very tasty liver of mullet; therefore that fish rose to such fortune that Asinius Celer, during the Empire of Claudius, paid eighty thousand nummi for one, which in our money is about one hundred fifty *scudi*.[19] Aristoxenus Cyrenaeus[20] sprinkled lettuce with honeydew water, in order to improve its taste. Sergius Orata, in Baia, was the first to invent oyster breeding, and Curtius of morays, and he brought six thousand to the triumphal dinner of Dictator Caesar. Lucullus excavated a mountain near Naples in order to make a salt water fishing pool on dry land, and it cost him more than his villa. After his death, the fish were sold for forty thousand golden sesterces, the equivalent of 400,000 ducats. Moreover, he fed different kinds of birds and wild animals, and the sumptuous banquets held in the Apolline (that apartment took its name from the statue of Apollo) surpassed all the others held until that time.

The banquets of Mark Anthony were famous, as that of Cleopatra in which a pearl of the value of one hundred thousand sesterces, equivalent to one million ducats, was eaten. This Queen was as proud as she was beautiful and was entertained every day by Mark Anthony. She criticised all things, however excellent they were, so he asked her what could be added to his banquets. She answered that she was going to spend one hundred thousand sesterces on a single dinner. He judged that such a thing was impossible, and he bet on this. On the appointed day, Cleopatra ordered a sumptuous and regal dinner, but not greater than those that Mark Anthony had presented to her. Laughing, he asked her to show to him on what she had spent that huge sum; she replied that before the dinner ended they were going to eat what she had said. When fruit was served, a Page, that had been so commanded, brought to the Queen a cup of very strong vinegar, whose strength liquefies

quando vennero le frutti, un Paggio, a cui era stato imposto, portò dinanzi alla Regina una Tazza di fortissimo[a] aceto, la cui forza liquefà le Perle. Havevano[b] due all'orecchie, le maggiori, et le più belle che fussero forse mai state viste, che glie l'haveva donate il Re d'Oriente, giudicata ciascuna di quelle, et maggior prezzo; ne spiccò una, et liquefatta la mangiò, et ponendo la mano all'altra per il medesimo effetto, Lucio / [p. 1661] Planco tra loro giudice eletto, giudicò haver vinto la Regina. Questa Perla, dapoiche Cleopatra morì, fù divisa per il mezo et ornava l'orecchie della statua di Venere nel Tempio Panteon hoggi detto la Ritonda.[c] Calligola nei suoi conviti usò dare per antipasto le Perle liquefatte; ma ciò non deve essere di maraviglia in un Imperator del Mondo, poiche Clodio d'Esopo, Histrione, havendo provato le Perle d'ottimo sapore, in una cena a ciascuno de convitati per antipasto ne diede a mangiare.

Piacquero tanto a Tiberio Cesare i Banchetti, che una volta stette due giorni, et una notte a Tavola / [p. 1662] et un' altra volta cenando a Casa di Clodio suo amico volse essere servito da fanciulle nude.

Vitellio nei suoi conviti mangiava tre volte il dì, et alcuna volta quattro, et sempre con diversi, et diverse vivande et, in ciascuna volta spendeva quattromillia numi d'oro,[d] il che sono 80/m ducati.

Famosissima fù la Cena che gli fece il fratello nella sua prima entrata in Roma, nella quale frà l'altre cose vi furono due millia elettiss[im]i pesci,[e] et settemillia uccelli, la quale però egli di gran lunga avanzò nel sacrificio et dedicatione della Palina a Giove, dove furono per antipasti in gran copia fegati / [p. 1663] di scauri,[f] latticinij di lamprede condotte dal Mar Carpatio oltre la Spagna, et cervella de Pavoni, et de Fagiani, et lingue de Pappagalli. Tutto questo si dimostra sotto il Re di Coppe, le quali si adoperano nelli conviti, così in porvi dentro vivande delicate, come anco preziosissimi vini.

Quindi considerando il savio Authore il corso della vita humana nelle delitie terrene in tutto aviluppata et per breve che sia senza giamai riempirsi, maggior cose sempre brama, le quali in poco d'hora nella Morte si perdono, et che tutto cio è una espressa et chiarissima pazzia in diverse belle figure / [p. 1664] inanzi agli occhi ce le pone acciocche conoscendo ciascuno le proprie passioni et li suoi errori, lasciando le vanità et li brevissimi et dannosi piaceri da parte alzi la mente alla contemplatione di Dio, et percio aggiunse al suo bellissimo

a B finissimo
b B Avevane
c B La Rotonda
d B quattromila scudi d'oro
e B due elettissimi Pesci (*missing* "millia")
f *Sic for* scari.

the pearl. At her ears she had two, possibly the greatest and most beautiful that had ever been seen, being a present of the King of the East, each of them was judged to have a greater value. She took one and she ate it liquefied. When she put her hand to the other to the same effect, Lucius Plancus, who had been elected as judge between them, judged that the Queen had won. That pearl, after the death of Cleopatra, was divided into two halves and it decorated the ears of the statue of Venus in the Pantheon temple, which is now called The Rotunda. In his banquets, Caligula gave liquefied pearls as a starter, but this is not a wonder for an Emperor of the World, since Clodius Esopus, an actor, having found that pearls had an excellent taste, gave them as a starter to each of the guests at one of his dinners.[21]

Tiberius Caesar loved banquets so much that he once spent two days and one night at table. Another time, dining at the house of his friend Clodius, he wanted to be served by naked girls.[22]

Vitellius in his banquets used to eat three times a day, and sometimes four; always with different people and different foods and every time he spent four thousand golden *nummi*, which amount to eighty thousand ducats.

The dinner that was offered to him by his brother at his first entrance into Rome is very famous: during it two thousand very choice fishes and seven thousand birds were served. But he greatly surpassed that in his sacrifices and dedication of the Palina[23] to Jove. The starters were a great abundance of parrotfish livers, young lampreys from the Carpathian Sea to beyond Spain, peacock and pheasant brains, parrot tongues.[24] All this is represented by the King of Cups, which are used in banquets, in order to serve both delicate foods and very precious wines.

The wise author considered how the course of human life is always entangled with mundane delights and, however short, it is never satisfied and always desires something more; and these things are lost in death in a very short time: all this is clear and manifest foolishness. He places those things before our eyes, with diverse beautiful figures, in order to make everyone know his passions and his errors and, leaving aside vanity and the very short and harmful pleasures, to raise his mind to the contemplation of God. Therefore he added to his most beautiful game XXII hieroglyphic figures[25] that represent different subjects, intending that, in the game, when void of cards of the four [suits], they should supply them. He called them triumphs, since they are affects and passions that triumph over men. Fifteen of them, together with the above described four professions, describe active life from

giuoco XXII figure hieroglifice[a] che rappresentano diversi oggetti, volendo nel giuoco che in difetto delle Carte dei quattro supplissero et chiamolli Trionfi, sendo proprij affetti, et passioni che degli huomini trionfano. Quindeci de quali insieme con le quattro professioni sopraditte[b] dal principio sino all' estremo fine della vita attiva dichiarano, et / [p. 1665] gli altri sette la contemplativa con il suo fine, ch' é Iddio. Diede ai primi per general Capitano il Matto, con tal conditione et privilegio che colui a chi tocca in sorte perdere non lo possa giamai se già tutto il giuoco non perde et benche faccia l'officio d'ogni carta non piglia et non è preso, volendo mostrare che tutti li difetti si possono perdere et lasciare, eccetto la pazzia della quale ognuno si tiene la sua sin che vive ; che il dare il Matto attorno far le Bergigole et dar la caccia al Bagattello et farlo all' ultimo sono giunte trovate da moderni per far mag[gio]re il giuoco. Gli pose appresso il Bagattello, percioche si come coloro, che / [p. 1666] con prestezza di mano giocando, una cosa per un' altra parer ci fanno, il che oltre alla maraviglia porge vana dilettatione, non essendo il suo fine altro che inganno cosi il Mondo allettando altrui sotto imagine di bello, et dilettevole promettendo contentezza, al fine da guai, et in guisa di prestigiatore non havendo in se cosa permanente ne durabile, con finta apparenza di bene, conduce a miserabil fine. Seguono due Papi, uno col Regno et l'altro senza et dopò[c] questi l'Imperatore, et il Re, che sono le due supreme dignità ; nello spirituale Cardinale et Papa, nel temporale Re, et Imperatore ; alle quali quasi / [p. 1667] per una scala di grado in grado non pur' i Preti et Cav[alie]ri et gli altri à loro superiori ma ogni altro ancora di minor conditione col pensiero, facendo come dir si suole, Castelli in aria, si ascende, ne mai si ferma che fra se stesso freneticando [sic] si fa del Mondo assoluto Padrone, et immortale. Et perche ancor' io con gli altri in schiera a freno sciolto corro dietro a questo pazzo, che volgendoci le spalle, et mostrandoci il sedere ci schernisce forza è poscia che io rida quando mi tiuouo [trovo] d'assoluto Monarcha, haver bisogno d'un scudo. Seguita poi la Prudenza in ordine e la fortezza la prima virtù dell' animo, l'altra del corpo ; et da molti / [p. 1668] estremamente desiderate. Percioche si trovano di quelli, che bramano d'essere in tutte le scienze universali, et perfetti senza havervi superiori, nè anco eguali, et percio esser tanto savii, che siano per nuovi Oracoli ammirati in Terra, saper tutte le cose non solamente le passate et le presenti ma le future ancora, et cosi gonfi d'ambitione et gloria commandare alle due dignità supreme, et governare il Mondo. Altri desiderano forze del corpo estreme, valore immenso et essere invicibili, onde soli potessero squarciare Leoni,

a B geroglifiche
b B con l' altre quattro professioni sopradette (*adds* "l'altre")
c B l'altro senza Regno, e doppo (*adds* "Regno")

its beginning to its extreme end, and the other seven describe contemplative life with its end, which is God. He assigned the Fool as the Captain of the first group, with such condition and privilege that whoever by chance receives it can never lose it, unless he loses the whole game: it can replace any other card, it does not capture and it is not captured. This shows that all defects can be lost and left, except for folly: everyone keeps his own as long as he lives. Presenting the Fool all around,[26] making combinations[27] and chasing the Bagat, and winning the last trick with it,[28] are all additions invented by modern players, in order to improve the game. He placed the Bagat next to him: because, like those that play with swift hands, making one thing look like another one, causing wonder and a vain amusement, since his only goal is deception, in the same way, the world attracts the others with images of beauty and delight, promising happiness at the end of trouble. As a juggler, it contains nothing either permanent, nor durable, and leads to a miserable end, under the false appearance of good. Two Popes follow, one with the reign [papal crown] and one without it. And after them the Emperor and the King, which are the highest dignities: in the spiritual, Cardinal and Pope, in the temporal, King and Emperor. Not only the Priests and Knights, and those superior to them, but all the others also of a lower condition, rise to them as along the steps of a stair, building in their thoughts, as one says, castles in the air; and one does not stop, and in his delirium he makes of himself the absolute and immortal Master of the World. And because I run free-reined, along with a bunch of others, behind this fool that, turning his shoulders to us, and showing his bottom, makes fun of us, therefore I must laugh when I find myself needing a *scudo*, instead of being an absolute monarch. In the order, Prudence follows, then Strength. The first is a virtue of the soul, the second of the body, and they are much desired by many. Because there are those who desire to be perfect and universal in all sciences, having neither superiors nor peers, being so wise that they are admired as new oracles on the earth. They want to know not only present and past things, but the future as well; inflated with ambition and glory, they want to have the two supreme dignities at their command and rule the world. Others desire the extreme strength of the body, an immense valour, being invincible, the only ones who can tear lions to pieces, kill snakes, defeat armies, conquer kingdoms and to be admired, feared and respected by all the trembling others. Those make themselves more prudent in their imagination, these stronger; they will be able to do more than what is convenient for reason, more than what all

occider Serpenti, vincere gli Esserciti, conquistare i / [p. 1669] Regni, et rendersi
à tutti ammirabili et tremebondi ; et per tali esser tenuti et reveriti, facendosi
con l'imaginatione quelli piu prudenti, et questi più forti via più di quanto per
ragione si conviene anzi più di quanto tutti gli huomini sono stati, et che saranno in un solo huomo uniti potranno fare, seguono l'insegna di questo
Capitano, qual' è un falcone che si becca i getti.

Ci sono appresso l'Amore, et il Carro et la Fortuna, tre potentissimi affetti humani. Amore è un' intenso desiderio di conseguir la cosa amata che da
bellezza nasce, in cui di maniera gli Amanti si infiammano / [p. 1670] che non
hanno ad alcuna sorte di pericoli per evidentissimi che sieno per giungere al
desiato fine, risguardo.

Sansone per gradire alla sua donna, li pose il capo in grembo, ed insegnol
il crine fatale, che gli fù poi cagione della perdita delle forze, della privatione
degli occhi,ᵃ et della vita insieme.

Il savio Salomone si lasciò con la briglia, et sella à guisa di bestia cavalcare.

Hercole si vesti da donna, et filò la lana. Leandro passavaᵇ il Mare, et al
fine vi si sommerse.

Et Cesare havendo vinto tutto il Mondo, fù dalle bellezze di Cleopatra
supe- / [p. 1671] rato, et dopò lui talmente Antonio, che non osò far cosa
mai, che fosse contro la sua voglia.

Varij sono stati li casi d'Amore, cosi nelle donne, come negli huomini, et
di varie pazzie, et folli ardim[en]ti pieni, et tanto grandi i desiderij degli
Amanti, che molte volte non potendo venire al desiderato fine, con le proprie
mani si sono date la morte, il che di rado negli altri casi occorre.

Per il Carro le superbe et lascive pompe del Mondo si dimostrano, cosi
nelle fabriche de Palazzi, et ornamenti di Tapezzarie, et pitture, et Vasi di
argento et d'oro lavorati di mirabili intagli, et gioie pieni, come nelle /
[p. 1672] publiche et private feste, et nel sontuoso, et superfluo vestire. Alle
Gentildonne Romane fù primieramente conceduta la Carretta, quando non si
potendo all'Oracolo sodisfare il voto di Camillo, portarono in Senato à gara
parte delle gioie et dell'oro, che havevano per loro uso, et ornamento, che
crebbero poi à poco à poco in si gran sfoggi, facendoli d'Ebano, et d'Avorio,
d'argento et d'oro con intagli et intarsiature di pietre preciose, che fù poi nec-
essario, essendo la spesa intolerabile, et la total rovina de Patritij per decreto
del Senato di levargliele di che esse adirate, et insieme fattone consiglio,
deliberorno [sic] di / [p. 1673] uccidere nel ventre i proprij figli, et più non

a B delle forze, della reputazione, della privazione degli occhi (*adds* "della reputazione")
b B passò

men have ever been or could be if united in a single man, following the device of this Captain, which is a falcon pecking his ties.

After this there are Love, the Chariot, and Fortune, three most powerful human affects. Love is an intense desire to obtain the desired thing. It is born from beauty. Lovers are so inflamed by it that they do not care about any kind of danger, however evident, in order to reach the desired end.

Samson, in order to please his woman, put his head on her lap, showing to her his fatal hair; this cost him the loss of strength, the privation of sight and life together.[29]

The wise Solomon suffered to be ridden like a beast, with reins and saddle.[30]

Hercules dressed like a woman and spun wool.[31] Leander swam the sea, and at the end was submerged in it.[32]

And Caesar, who had won the whole world, was conquered by the beauties of Cleopatra, and after him Anthony, who never dared to do anything against her will.[33]

The vicissitudes of love have been various, for both women and men, full of various follies and crazy temerity. The desire of lovers has been so great that many times, when they could not reach the desired end, they killed themselves with their own hands, which in other cases seldom occurs. The Chariot represents the superb and lavish luxury of the world, in the architecture of buildings, and the decoration of tapestry, and paintings, and in golden and silver vases, adorned with wonderful engravings and full of jewels; as also in public and private feasts, and sumptuous and superfluous clothes. The cart was firstly conceded to the Roman women:[34] when the vow of Camillus to the oracle could not be satisfied, they competed to bring to the Senate a part of the jewels and gold that they had for their use and ornament. They gradually grew in such great displays, making them of ebony, ivory, silver and gold with engravings and inlays of precious stones that it was necessary – the expense being unsustainable, to the total ruin of the Patricians – to take away those things by means of a decree of the Senate. They were so angry for this that, taking counsel together, they decided to kill their children in their wombs, not giving birth anymore, so that the senatorial blood should come to an end. Therefore, in a short time, they noticed the malignity and obstinacy of their women and were forced to give back those things. From this we clearly know that one must expect a harsh revenge when taking away that which they have once put to use

partorire, perché venisse il sangue senatorio a meno, onde in processo di poco tempo accortisi della maligna ostinatione delle lor donne, furono forzati di restituirgliele, da che chiaramente si conosce, che non bisogna torle senza aspettatione d'aspra vendetta quello che per accrescer la pompa, et le bellezze loro hanno posto una volta in uso con tutto, che se ne vedesse un comune, et manifesto pregiudicio.

Agrippina Moglie di Claudio Imp[erato]re vestiva vesti fatte tutte d'oro senza altre misture piene di gioie di infinito valore. Lollia Paolina moglie di Calligola, non dico quando / [p. 1674] solennemente in qualche gran cerimonia, et festa si adornava, ma quando andava alle cene di mediocri sponsalitij, era coperta di tante et sì belle Perle et smeraldi, che tutto il capo rilucevano distinti con vago ordine ne capelli negli occhi, nel collo, et nelle dita che ascendevano alla valuta di quattro cento millia sestertij d'oro,[a] che importano quattro millioni di ducati, et diceva ch'era sempre pronta a provare per scritture questa valuta.

Ma che diremo dell'uso degli huomini, certo, che hanno avanzato la leggerezza et vana gloria delle donne. Cesare ebbe una Corazza di Perle / [p. 1675] la quale dedicò poi a Venere genitrice, et nei giuochi funebri del Padre fece tutto l'apparato d'argento.

Marcantonio fece recitare una Comedia in scena d'argento, et Nerone fece coprire d'oro il Teatro di Pompeo quando lo mostrò al Re d'Armenia, et pescava colle reti d'oro, et fune di purpura.

Eliogabalo caminava sopra l'oro quando andava da Palazzo al Tempio. Pompeo Magno nel trionfo della vittoria delli Pirati, et del Re di Ponto nel di ultimo di settembre, qual' era il suo natale mostrò un Tavoliere d'oro largo due piedi, et lungo quattro, con le tavole di due bellissime gioie, et una lucerna d'oro di trenta [p. 1676] libre, et tre Tavole da mangiare d'oro, [e credenze di vasi d'oro][b] et pietre preciose, le statue di Minerva, d'Apollo, et di Marte d'oro et un Monte quadro d'oro, con Cervi et Cani et d'ogni sorte pomi d'oro.[c] Un Museo di Perle, nella sommità del quale era un' Orologio, e la sua statua d'oro con la faccia di Perle et sei bellissimi[d] vasi di Mirrina, che consecró à Giove, della qual materia si fecero poi Tavole, et vasi da mangiare, et da bere, di che crebbe in modo il preggio che Tito Petronio huomo consolare haveva una Tazza mirrina di valore di tre millia scudi, et una n' hebbe Nerone di quattro milia.

a B quattromila sestertij d'oro
b B; missing in A.
c B ogni sorte di pomi (adds "di")
d B un museo di perle, e sei bellissimi (*missing* "nella sommità ... la faccia di Perle")

in order to increase their pomp and beauty, even if a common and evident damage results from it.

Agrippina, wife of Emperor Claudius, wore clothes that were entirely made of gold, without any other mixture, full of jewels of infinite value.[35] Lollia Paulina, wife of Caligula, not only when she adorned herself for some great celebration or festivity, but also when she went to a mediocre marriage, was covered with such beautiful pearls and emeralds that they shone all over her head with a beautiful order, on her hair, eyes, neck and fingers. They had the value of four hundred thousand golden sesterces, which corresponded to four millions ducats. And she said that she was always ready to guarantee by writing such an amount of money.[36]

But what shall we say about the habits of men? Certainly, that they surpassed the thoughtlessness and vainglory of women. Caesar had armour made of pearls, that later he dedicated to Venus as his ancestor.[37] In the funeral games for his father, he made all the decorations of silver. Mark Anthony had a comedy represented on a stage of silver. And Nero had the Theatre of Pompey covered with gold, when he presented it to the King of Armenia;[38] he used to fish with golden nets and purple ropes.[39]

Heliogabalus walked on gold when he went from his palace to the temple.[40] Pompey the Great, in the triumph for his victories over the Pirates and the King of Pontus, on the last day of September, which was his birthday, displayed a table two feet wide and four long, with two beautiful jewels on the top, and a golden lamp weighing thirty pounds, and three eating tables made of gold, and cupboards of golden vases, and precious stones, and golden statues of Minerva, Apollo and Mars, a square mountain of gold, with deer, dogs and every kind of fruit made of gold, a museum of pearls, at the top of which there was a clock, and his golden statue with the face made of pearls and six beautiful murrhine vases, which he dedicated to Jove.[41] Later from that material eating tables and drinking vases were made; its price grew so much that the consul Titus Petronius had a murrhine cup with a value of three thousand *scudi*, and Nero had one worth four thousand.

This murrhine was thought to be a condensation of the hot humour that is under the earth. It is beautiful for its variety, because it is lucid and shining, with floating spots, some almost purple, others transparent, and others of a mix of the two, with reflexes on the edges that are similar to a rainbow. In our times, there are contemporary people who follow as much as they can the foolishness of the ancients, in accumulating treasure, and being very

Questa Mirrina si stimava che fusse d'humore dal / [p. 1677] caldo sotto terra condensato, vaga per la sua varietà, perche era lucida et risplendente et per entro vi ondeggiavano macchie, che tiravano alla porpora, et altre al cristallino, et altre ad un misto d'ambedue con certe riverberazioni nell'estremità a guisa d'Arco celeste. Non mancano anco a' tempi nostri de moderni, che in quanto possono le pazzie degli antichi seguono così nell'accumular Tesori, et essere avarissimi, come nel superfluo vivere et vestire, et altri sfarzi troppo estremi.

La fortuna si hà acquistato in opinione di molti deità, onde dagli antichi gli furono sacrati Tempij, et per / [p. 1678] Dea reverita, come da lei ogni infortunio et felicità dipende; et perciò sono molti che in lei si buttano ogni colpa d'ogni loro sinistro, et malo evento, et da lei tutto quello, che di bene, che gli avviene riconoscono, reputandosi nelle loro attioni hor fortunati, hor sfortunati secondo il successo delle cose. Il che tra' tutti gli altri si ode ogni di tra' Corteggiani, quali se considerassino alla servitù che fanno, et alla natura de Sig[no]ri a chi servono, ragionevolmente parlando, non possono dire né l'uno, né l'altro, percioche chi mal serve dolgasi di se stesso, che non merita, et non della fortuna : et se la lunga servitù è tale, che meriti risguardo / [p. 1679] et remuneratione, et pur non l'habbia dolgasi del Sig[no]re in cui ha male impiegato i suoi servitij, che non ci ha colpa la fortuna s'egli è avaro, ingrato, et inconsiderato. Et se avviene, che pure spesso si vede, che si doni a' chi manco merita, et men serve, et meno si deve, non nasce da fortuna, ma da impeto violento da occulta similitudine causato ch'è tra loro, operando a guisa di calamita, che lascia l'argento et l'oro, odia il diamante, et trova il ferro.

Hor dopo questi segue il Gobbo, il Traditore, la Morte, et il Diavolo. Per il Gobbo, che altro non è che il Tempo ci si mostra, che tutte queste sono vane et transitorie ; et percio soma / [p. 1680] pazzia è ad amarle et desiderarle tanto intensamente, che ad altro non pensi poiche in poco d'hora giunge la Vecchiaia da tutte le miserie accompagnata, et allhora si cominciano a conoscere l'inganni dell' assassino Mondo, postoci avanti agli occhi per il Traditore. Ma havendoci fatto sopra durissimo callo, et l'habito tristo, et malagevole a potersene ritirare senza punto allontanarsi dagli usati errori, sopraviene all' improviso la Morte, nell' horror della quale sbigottiti, et disperati il Diavolo, che di tutto cio è stato cagione se gli porta via. Et questo è il miserabil fine dell' attioni humane, di coloro dico che / [p. 1681] immersi totalmente nelle vane et lascive delitie, che promette et può dare il Mondo, seguendo per guida la pazzia, non hanno mai risguardo al suo fine, et à Dio ; da cui solo nasce et dipende il vero et sommo bene, et felicità perfetta et permanente. La contemplation del quale ci dimostra per l'opere sue mar-

greedy, as well as in a life full of superfluous things and an excess of extreme luxury.

In the opinion of many, fortune has been made a divinity, the Ancients dedicating sacred temples to her and revering her has a Goddess, because all troubles and happiness depend on her. Therefore there are many that attribute to her the causes of all their unhappy and troublesome events as well as of everything good that happens to them, considering themselves fortunate or unfortunate according to the outcome of things. This is mainly heard every day from courtiers. If they considered the service they provide, and the nature of the lords they serve, they could not reasonably say either one thing or the other. Someone who offers a bad service should blame himself, not fortune, that he is not deserving. And if a long service deserves respect and reward and does not receive any, one should blame the Lord to whom all service has been dedicated in vain: fortune has no fault for his being greedy, ungrateful and inconsiderate. If it often happens, as we see, that he who is not worthy, and less useful, and even less deserving, is rewarded, this is not due to fortune, but to the strong impetus of a hidden affinity among people, with results similar to those of a magnet, that ignores silver and gold, hates diamonds, and finds iron.

After these, the Hunchback, the Traitor, Death and the Devil follow. The Hunchback, who is none other than Time, demonstrates that all those things are vain and transitory. Therefore loving and desiring them so intensely, thinking of nothing else, is the greatest foolishness, because in a short time Old Age comes together with all its miseries: then people begin to understand the deceptions of the murderous World, which are put before our eyes by the Traitor. But since they have gotten so used to their bad habits, it is difficult to get free of them: they do not depart from their usual errors. Suddenly Death comes, in the horror of which the Devil, who is the cause of all this, takes them away in fright and despair. This is the miserable end of human actions, speaking of those who are completely immersed in the vain and lascivious delights that the World promises and can give: they follow foolishness as their guide, without regard to their end and to God, upon whom the greatest good and all perfect and permanent happiness depend. His contemplation is wisely presented by the Author in the following seven figures by means of his marvellous and beautiful works, so that, knowing him, we love him. So that, for his infinite goodness and mercy, he delivers us from the Devil at the end of our lives, making us co-heirs with him of his true glory, and the happiness of Heaven.[42] Therefore we rise with

avigliose, et belle dottamente l'Auttore nelle sette figure[a] seguenti, accioche conoscendolo l'amiamo. Onde egli per sua infinita bontà, et misericordia nel fine della vita nostra dalle mani del Diavolo ci sottragga, et ci faccia seco coheredi della vera sua gloria, et felicità del Cielo, et quindi accrescendo et con / [p. 1682] gli occhi et con l'intelletto ai Cieli, la Stella, la Luna, et il Sole, le sopranaturali fatture de Dio, cosi nello stellato, et fisso come nei mobili Pianeti il Mondo, de quali dalla propria di ciascuno intelligenza depende ch'è l'Angelo, il quale li governa, et muove in virtù del primo Motore, ch' è il grande et immortale Iddio rappresentato per la Giustizia, percioche nel giorno del Guidicio si mostrera giustiss[im]o Giudice et severo retribuendo a ciascuno secondo l'opere sue.

L'ultima figura è il Mondo di niente da lui fatto, il quale si come ogni cosa comprende, cosi anco questo giuoco conchiude,[b] il / [p. 1683] quale è una vera imagine et ritratto del naturale di tutto quello, che nell' huomo, il quale è un picciol mondo, si contiene.

a B nelle sue figure
b B questo gioco (*missing* "conchiude")

our eyes and intellects to the Heavens, the Star, the Moon and the Sun, the supernatural creatures of God, the World, so in the fixed stars as in the mobile Planets. Each of them depends on its own intelligence which is the Angel, who governs and moves them, in virtue of the first Mover, who is the great and immortal God. He is represented by Justice, because at Judgement day he will be a most righteous and severe Judge, repaying everyone according to their deeds.

The last figure is the World, which he created from nothing; since it includes everything, it also includes this game, which is a true image and portrait of the nature of all that is contained in man, who is a little world.

Notes and Comments to the Anonymous *Discorso*

1 The duality of the *vita activa* and *vita contemplativa* hearkens from classical times, becoming a medieval and scholastic commonplace, for instance explored by Thomas Aquinas in his *Summa Theologica* (II-II a. 1, q. 182; IIIa q. 40 a. 1 ad 2). It became important in the thinking of early humanists such as Coluccio Salutati (1331-1406; see e.g. Victoria Kahn, "Coluccio Salutati on the Active and Contemplative Lives", in Brian Vickers, ed., *Arbeit, Musse, Meditation: Betrachtungen zur "Vita activa" und "Vita contemplativa"* (Zurich, 1985), pp. 153-179), while later in the 15th century Cristoforo Landino devoted Book I of his influential *Disputationes Camaldulenses* ("De vita activa et contemplativa"), c. 1474, to the two ways of life (see e.g. Bruce G. McNair, "Cristoforo Landino and Coluccio Salutati on the Best of Life", *Renaissance Quarterly*, 47, no. 4 (1994), pp. 747-769). Our author was alluding to an ongoing discussion that was common knowledge to his audience.

2 Marco Girolamo Vida (c. 1480-1566), *Guerra del giuoco degli scacchi, voltata d'heroici, in versi sciolti,* Rome, 1544 (Zollinger 1996, no. 895*), Italian translation of *Scacchia ludus,* written around 1510, printed in 1525 (Zollinger 1996, no. 890): see *The game of chess. Marco Girolamo Viida's Scacchia ludus,* M. di Cesare, ed., Nieuwkoop, 1975, and J. Chomarat, "Les échecs d'après Vida", in *Les jeux à la Renaissance,* Paris, 1982, pp. 367-81. On chess, besides Vida, the author could read Damiano da Odemira, *Questo libro e da imparare giocare a scacchi e de le partiti,* Rome, 1512 (Zollinger 1996, no. 5), repr. 1518 (Zollinger 1996, no. 7), 1524/25 (Zollinger 1996, no. 9), etc. (undated editions between 1525 and 1540: Zollinger 1996, nos. 10, 13, 14, 16, 19), then Venice, 1564 (Zollinger 1996, no. 30). The book by Ruy Lopez de Sigura, *Libro de la invencion liberal y arte del juego del axedrez,* printed in Alcala (Spain) in 1561, Ital. transl. 1584 (*Il giuoco de gli scacchi di Rui Lopez, Spagnuolo, nuovamente tradotto in lingua italiana da M. Gio. Domenico Tarsia,* Venice, 1584), was probably too late for the author.

3 Galen's treatise on the ball game was translated from Greek to Latin and printed in Venice in 1533 (Zollinger 1996, no. 658), then translated from Latin to Italian in Milan in 1562 as *Il libro di Claudio Galeno Dell'esercizio della palla nuovamente tradotto della lingua Latina nella nostra volgare,* Milan, 1562 (Zollinger 1996, no. 710). This Italian edition seems to be the latest work the *Discorso* alludes to. Besides Galen's book, there was also Antonio Scaino, *Trattato del giuoco della palla,* Venice, 1555 (Zollinger 1996, no. 21).

4 Obviously the author had not heard of Francesco Piscina's *Discorso sopra l'ordine delle figure dei Tarocchi* (Mondovì, 1565), a work whose circulation seems to have been very limited and which was printed far from the place where the present *Discorso* was being written. For Piscina see Part I.

5 It is strange to find *mazze* for *bastoni* here. Normally it is a southern (Naples and Sicily) regional use; however, we have found that a poem included in a 16th-century anonymous musical manuscript compiled near Pesaro and now kept in the Pesaro City Library, also uses *mazze* in the same meaning. Therefore *mazze* was also understood in the Pesaro area. See Introduction.

6 This statement agrees with the earliest known indication of a "rule" for playing Tarot, in Ugo Trotti, *De multiplici ludo,* written in Ferrara in 1456, who praises the game since it "has more skill than fortune, as when four play Triumphs in pairs" ("plus habet industrie quam fortune veluti si quatuor bipertiti ludunt ad triumphos"). See Gherardo Ortalli, "The Prince and the Playing Cards", *Ludica* 2 (1996), p. 199 n. 105.

7 Greek τάριχος "salty sauce".

8 This unusual claim was independently asserted later by some early historians of playing cards. A contemporary of our author, Lambert Daneau, made the same claim in 1566 in his *Brieve remonstrance sur les jeux de sort ou de hasard.*

9 The philosophy of Epicurus was known directly from Book X of Diogenes Laertius' *Lives and Opinions of Eminent Philosophers,* as well as indirectly by the testimony of many classical and medieval authors. The first Latin translation was made by Ambrogio Traversari around 1432.

10 *Canzoniere,* 7.

11 Horace, *Epistolarum,* lib. I, ep. i, ll. 53-54 ('ad Maecenatem'): "O cives, cives, quaerenda pecunia primum est, Virtus post nummos". English transl. by C. Smart, *The Works of Horace, translated literally into English prose* (5th ed., London, 1780), vol. II, pp. 178-179 (found on Google Books): "O citizens, citizens, wealth is to be sought for first, virtue after riches."

12 Virgil, *Aeneid* III. 49-57; Ovid, *Metamorphoses* XIII, 432ff; and others.

13 Virgil, *Aeneid* I, 350ff.

14 Marcus Porcius Cato Uticensis, c. 95-46 BC, Roman politician; the wife in question is Marcia. Quintus Hortensius Hortalus, c. 114-50 BC, orator. For this story see Plutarch, *Cato the Younger (Cato Minor),* c. 52, 3-5.

15 Pliny the Elder, *Natural History (NH),* XXXIII, 5.

16 This line is supposed to have been pronounced by the King of Parthia Orodes after he had captured Crassus (Marcus Licinius Crassus Dives, c. 115-53 BC) at the battle of Carrhae and beheaded him, pouring liquid gold into his mouth, thus satirizing Crassus' well-known thirst for gold. Many modern editors, and particularly Dante scholars claim that the Latin original version, "Aurum sitisti aurum bibe", is quoted in Cicero's *De Officiis,* I, 30 (and sometimes also II, 17, 18, or II, 57...), unless it is in *De Finibus bonorum et malorum,* III, xxii. Many refer also to Florus (*Epitome de Gestis Romanorum Historiarum...,* III, 11), or even to Greek-speaking historians like Cassius

Dio or Appian. However, as Paolo Garbini, "L'«*exemplum*» di Crasso: *Purgatorio*, XX 116-17", *Filologia e Critica*, XVI, 1991, II, pp. 272-6, has brilliantly demonstrated, none of these authors, and certainly not Cicero, uses this phrase. The nearest one can find is the 2nd-century Roman historian Lucius Annaeus Florus, but, although he tells the story of Crassus' terrible end, he does not cite any particular sentence. Garbini has shown that the Latin quote came from Vincent de Beauvais' *Speculum morale* (actually compiled around 1300 by a follower), where it can be read in III 7, 2. Medieval commentators of Dante's *Purgatorio* have all explained the verses "Ultimamente ci si grida: o Crasso / Dilci, ché 'l sai, di che sapore è l'oro" (*Purg.*, XX, v. 116-117), by recalling the story of Crassus' death and concluding it with the famous sentence. Among these some, writing in Italian, quoted the sentence as "d'oro avesti sete, ed oro bei e saziati" (*Ottimo commento*), or "Tu ài avuto sete dell'oro, et oro bei" (Francesco da Buti); Cristoforo Landino's own commentary on *Purgatorio* (*La divina comedia cum comento di Christophoro Landino*, Venice, 1481, and later reprints) has: "Fugli dipoi taglato la testa, et messo in uno otro d'oro structo, et dectogli: 'oro setisti, oro bei'." It is perhaps from here that our Anonymous got it.

17 *Aeneid*, III, 56-7: "Quod non mortalia pectora cogis, auri sacra fames?," which was translated by Dante as "Perche non reggi tu, o sacra fame dell' oro" (*Purg.*, XXII, 41). We can see that the Anonymous does not use Dante's words, but perhaps a paraphrase of his own.

18 This is the celebrated "Sardanapalus Epitaph", for a legendary king of Nineveh who allegedly had this Epicurean sentence engraved on his tomb; many Greek and Roman authors (Aristotle, Polybius, Diodorus of Sicily, Strabo, Dio Chrysostom, Cicero, etc.) report it in various versions: "Ede, bibe, lude, post mortem nulla voluptas" seems to be the closest Latin form to this Italian quotation. These very words can be found verbatim in *La difesa per le donne* by Vicenzo Sigonio, composed between 1556 and 1560, Cap. 21 ('Che le donne non sono golose né dedite al vino'): "Mangia, bevi e gioca, che dopo morte non è piacere alcuno". Since this text was only published in the 20th century (edizione critica a cura di Fabio Marri, Bologna, 1978), one may wonder whether our Anonymous had seen a copy.

19 Pliny, *NH* IX, 31, here in its Italian translation by Cristoforo Landino (1476), copied verbatim (cf. *Historia naturale di C. Plinio Secondo, di lingua latina in fiorentina tradocta per Christophoro Landino fiorentino,* Venice, 1534, p. CLXXXVI). The *scudi* conversion is an addition by the author of the *Discorso*.

20 'Aristossene Cireneo' (i.e. Aristoxenus of Cyrene, or Cyrenaeus) was a Greek philosopher and gourmet (not to be confused with Aristoxenus of Tarantum). He appears, as Aristosseno Cireneo, in Ortensio Lando, 'Catalogo de gl'inventori delle cose che si mangiano e delle bevande ch'oggidi s'usano', in *Commentario delle più notabili & mostruose cose d'Italia & altri luoghi di lingua aramea in italiana tradotto,*

con un breve catalogo de gli inventori delle cose che si mangiano & beveno, Venice, 1548 (and later reprints in 1550, 1553, 1554, 1569), annotated modern edn. (of the 1553 printing) by Guido & Paola Salvatori, Bologna, 1994, p. 130. Sergio Orata (Sergius Aurata, *fl.* c. 95 BC) pioneered the breeding and trade of oysters and is credited with the invention of the hypocaust at Baia/Baiae (see his Wikipedia entry under 'Sergius Orata'). His story may also come from Lando (see quoted edn., p. 108).

21 Pliny, *NH* IX, 58-59. The author of the *Discorso* closely follows the Italian translation by Cristoforo Landino, printed in Venice in 1476 and many times reprinted. It is our author, though, who adds the Pantheon is also called "today" 'la Ritonda', an appellation that was already known to Vasari (*Vite*, Introduzione, 1547). Note that the Bologna manuscript has the more standard 'Rotonda'. Clodius' extravagant act is also described by Horace, *Satires* II, iii, 239-242.

22 Suetonius, *The Lives of the Twelve Caesars,* "Life of Tiberius", 42. This "Clodius" is not to be confused with "Clodius the actor" mentioned above. Del Rosso''s translation of Suetonius, *Le Vite de dodici Cesari di Gaio Suetonio Tranquillo. Tradotte in lingua toscana per m. Paolo Del Rosso cittadino fiorentino*, Rome, 1544, reports that it was at the house of Sesto Claudio that Tiberius demanded to be waited upon by the "usual custom" of nude girls. Other versions of Suetonius have Sestio or Cestio Gallo (i.e. Caius Cestius Gallus, consul in AD 35) in this place.

23 For Vitellius dedicating something called "the Palina" to Jupiter we can find no source. Del Rosso appears to have translated Minerva's shield (ἀιγίδα) πολιούχου as "padrone della città", which he or the anonymous must have then interpreted as Jupiter, since Jupiter Capitolinus was the central temple and the aegis was Jupiter's shield (as well as Minerva's). The word *palina* must be an error for *patina*.

24 Suetonius, *The Lives of the Twelve Caesars*, "Life of Vitellius", chap. 13. But our *Discorso* does not seem to follow Del Rosso's translation here.

25 The term *hieroglifice* is used here as meaning "sacred and enigmatic images". Egyptian hieroglyphs were the object of an extreme curiosity by Renaissance humanists. Re-discovered in 1422 the 5th-century treatise *Hieroglyphica* by one 'Horapollo' (or Horus Apollo) was first printed in 1505 and reprinted many times in the following years, including an Italian translation (*Oro Apolline Niliaco, Delli segni hierogliphici*, Venice, 1547). Before their deciphering by Champollion (1822), hieroglyphs were thought to be an ancient symbolic language whose moral content anticipated the Christian message.

26 *dare il Matto attorno*, a phrase we have found nowhere else and whose meaning still puzzles us.

27 *far le Bergigole;* we understand here *bergigole* (sg. *bergigola*) as a regional version of *versicola, verzicola*, a term used in Minchiate – the Florentine form of Tarot – for various sets of high or low consecutive trumps, or sets of courts, of major trumps,

etc. Piscina uses it too – as *brezicola* (see Part I) – but with a slightly different meaning: in Piedmont, it obviously indicated the gathering of all four courts of the same suit. The nearest form we have found today, *barzigola* or *berzigola,* is used in Emilia as a word for marinated and grilled mutton.

28 *dar la caccia al Bagattello et farlo all' ultimo;* these two actions are well-known favourites of modern Tarot players. These phrases will be immediately recognized by modern French players when quite literally translated, as "chasse au petit" and "petit au bout." The anonymous author suggests these two options, together with the preceding ones, were recently introduced into the game. It is a fact that neither Flavio Alberto Lollio in his *Invettiva contra il giuoco del tarocco* (1550) nor Vincenzo Imperiali in his *Risposta* to Lollio mention any of these options. According to Dummett & McLeod 2004 (p. 33), a bonus for winning the last trick with the Bagatto (known in German-speaking countries as 'Pagat ultimo') was unknown in Italy, save in the Piedmontese three-hand game Mitigati (18th century). Recalling that "The idea of the Bagatto ultimo is wholly absent from those Tarot games played in Italy which we know to be free of foreign influence", they conclude: "It was certainly not in Italy that this important invention occurred, but either in Germany or, slightly less probably, in France." We can see here that it was in fact introduced, somewhere in an Italian region under Ferrarese influence, as early as the second half of the 16th century. However, it does not seem to have spread widely, but the feature is indeed characteristic of the French and German styles of play. For Dummett & McLeod it was "originally developed for the three-handed game".

29 The biblical story of Samson and Delilah is told in the book of *Judges*, chapter 16 vv. 1-18.

30 No such story is told of Solomon in the Bible, nor in any apocryphal or pseudepigraphal texts; it is not in any of the medieval collections of exempla, nor is it a Jewish legend. It could be a metaphorical reading of Solomon's bondage to his foreign wives (I *Kings* 11) or a reference to the *Song of Songs*, also known as the *Song of Solomon*. However, it seems much more likely that the author conflated wise Solomon with another famously wise man, Aristotle, as told in the popular medieval tale of 'Phyllis and Aristotle', apparently invented by the 13th-century Norman poet Henri d'Andeli as *Le lai d'Aristote*, in which exactly such a scene takes place. The story was frequently retold and represented in art, sometimes (in Italy) beside representations of Solomon and his wives, for at least three centuries, becoming a canonical icon of the power of love.

31 During Hercules' servitude to Omphale, Queen of Lydia; see e.g. Ovid, *Fasti* II, 305ff (Februrary 15, *Lupercalia*), and Ovid, *Heroides* IX, 53ff.

32 The story of Leander and Hero; see, chiefly, Musaeus, *De Herone et Leandro;* Ovid, *Heroides* XVIII.

33 For Caesar with Cleopatra, see e.g. Suetonius, *Life of Julius Caesar,* 52; Plutarch, *Life of Julius Caesar,* 48-49; for Anthony, Plutarch, *Life of Anthony,* 10, 25ff.

34 From Livy, *History of Rome,* Book V, 25. Roman matrons supplied part of the gold necessary to accomplish the vow pronounced by dictator Marcus Furius Camillus during the siege of Veii. The senate, as a sign of gratitude, granted them the honour of going to sacred festivals and games in carriages.

35 Pliny, *NH*, XXXIII, 19.

36 Pliny, *NH*, IX, 58. Here again quoted from Landino's translation (1534 printing, p. XXXIII, 16).

37 Pliny, *NH*, IX, 57.

38 All this comes from Pliny, *NH*, XXXIII, 16, mostly in the words of Landino's translation, 1534 printing, p. DCCV, right hand column.

39 Suetonius, *Life of Nero*, 30, 3.

40 Herodian, *Roman History*, V, vi, 8; cf. *Historia Augusta (Augustan History),* "Life of Elagabalus", 31, 8.

41 Narrative of Pompey's third triumph as in Pliny, *NH*, XXXVII "On stones", cap. vi, here too according to Landino's Italian translation.

42 *del Cielo;* This title for the card is paralleled in Vincenzo Imperiali's *Risposta* to Alberto Lollio's *Invettiva contra il giuoco del tarocco* (1550), line 263, which also follows the B order. Other lists of the B order call it Saetta, Fuoco, or Casa (del Diavolo). For a recent transcription of Lollio's *Invettiva* and Imperiali's *Risposta*, see Zorli 2010.

Bibliography

Berti/Vitali 1987: Giordano Berti, Andrea Vitali (eds.), *Le carte di corte : I tarocchi. Gioco e magia alla corte degli Estense,* Bologna : Nuova Alfa Editoriale, 1987 (exhibition catalogue).

Bruni 1992: Francesco Bruni (ed.), *L'italiano nelle regioni : Lingua nazionale e identità regionali,* Turin : UTET, 1992.

Bruni 1994: Francesco Bruni (ed.), *L'italiano nelle regioni : Testi e documenti,* Turin : UTET, 1994.

Depaulis 2002: Thierry Depaulis, "Quand l'abbé de Marolles jouait au tarot", *Le Vieux Papier,* fasc. 365, July 2002, pp. 313-326.

Depaulis 2005: Thierry Depaulis, *Cartes et cartiers dans les anciens États de Savoie (1400-1860)*, North Walsham : International Playing-Card Society, 2005 (IPCS Papers, 4).

Devoto/Giacomelli 1972: Giacomo Devoto, Gabriella Giacomelli, *I dialetti delle regioni d'Italia*, Florence : Sansoni, 1972.

Dummett 1980: Michael Dummett, *The Game of Tarot*, London : Duckworth, 1980.

Dummett 1993: Michael Dummett, *Il Mondo e l'Angelo : i tarocchi e la loro storia*, Naples : Bibliopolis, 1993

Dummett/McLeod 2004: Michael Dummett, John McLeod, *A History of Games Played with the Tarot Pack : The Game of Triumphs*, 2 vol., Lampeter, Ceredigion : Edwin Mellen Press, 2004.

Kaplan 1978: Stuart R. Kaplan, *The Encyclopedia of Tarot*, New York : U.S. Games Systems, 1978.

Kaplan 1986: Stuart R. Kaplan, *The Encyclopedia of Tarot*, (II), New York : U.S. Games Systems, 1986.

Little 1999: Tom Tadfor Little, "The Early Ordering of the Trumps", webpage at www.tarothermit.com/ordering.htm, and "The Classification of Tarot Designs", webpage at www.tarothermit.com/lineage.htm, both ©1999, accessed 15/01/2010.

Nadin 1997: Lucia Nadin, *Carte da gioco e letteratura tra Quattrocento e Ottocento*, Lucca : Maria Pacini Fazzi, 1997.

Piscina/Berti 1995: Francesco Piscina, *Discorso sopra l'ordine delle figure dei Tarocchi*, facsimile reprint, with an introduction by Giordano Berti, Bologna : Istituto Graf, 1995.

Pratesi 1987a: Franco Pratesi, "Italian cards, new discoveries, 2: An early praise of Italian tarot in the 16th century", *The Playing-Card*, XV-3, Feb. 1987, pp. 80-87.

Pratesi 1987b: Franco Pratesi, "Italian cards, new discoveries, 3: Ferrarese tarot in the 16th century, invective and answer", *The Playing-Card*, XV-4, May 1987, pp. 123-131.

Pratesi 1987c: Franco Pratesi, "Italian cards, new discoveries, 4: Tarot in Piedmont in the XVIth century : the oldest book on the subject", *The Playing-Card*, XVI-1, Aug. 1987, pp. 27-36.

Zollinger 1996: Manfred Zollinger, *Bibliographie der Spielbücher des 15. bis 18. Jahrhunderts*, Erster Band : *1473-1700*, Stuttgart : Anton Hiersemann, 1996 (Hiersemanns bibliographische Handbücher, Bd. 12).

Zorli 2010: a transcription of Lollio's *Invettiva* and Imperiali's *Risposta*, downloadable pdf file at www.tretre.it/index.php?id=200&L=0

Index

www.ingramcontent.com/pod-product-compliance
Lightning Source LLC
Chambersburg PA
CBHW070317290526
45791CB00003B/1140